SERIOUSLY...
WHAT AM I DOING HERE?

SERIOUSLY...
WHAT AM I DOING HERE?

**The Adventures of a Wondering
and Wandering Gay Jew**

Ken Schneck
Art by Dave Perillo

For Gran (Alice Bessen): You ended every conversation with "And that's all, Kenneth?" You challenged me to do more, give more, and be more.

CONTENTS

INTRODUCTION

I am not an adventurer.

Far from it.

My family spent vacations almost exclusively at myriad Club Meds: a whopping four of them. Although my siblings and I were assured that each Club Med was located in a different country from the previous one, they all could have been situated on a tropical resort movie set in Kissimmee, Florida; each Club Med was a carbon copy of the others. Everything was identical: from their drink currency of orange and yellow beads (do they still have those?!) to the endless loop of "Hands Up," Club Med's inescapable-yet-endlessly entertaining anthem piped through any palm tree that could hold a speaker.

My family never went camping. We never even came close. Okay, there was that one time when a salamander crawled under the door in our hotel room. Panic ensued. From that vacation on, we stuffed towels under hotel doors lest any future amphibians get the wrong idea about the Schneck brand of hospitality. Other than that singular encounter with nature, I honestly don't think we even left a window open in a hotel room overnight.

We never did circus-like activities. Okay, there was that one time when I was in an actual circus show (*see above: Club Med*). But I was the bellowing ringmaster in a top hat and a painted-on mustache, not the performer in any of the actual death-defying acts like the lady who did cartwheels or the guy who almost juggled four balls at the same time. Almost.

We never braved the elements. Okay, there was that one time when we got caught outside in the rain in California. But we were in Disneyland. Salvation came in the form of an indoor screening of *Captain EO*, so our one day at "The Happiest Place on Earth" wasn't a total washout. Michael Jackson and 3-D glasses in the dry inside will beat out Adventureland in the wet outside any day of the week.

In my teens and twenties, I never strayed too far from home to explore the world. New York City was my playground. And, by "New York City," I mean Manhattan, below 16th Street. I had heard a tale that there were four other boroughs to explore. This was a myth that was often repeated in hushed tones in backrooms but one I had never actually been able to confirm. Furthermore, New York City was only a seventeen-minute car ride away from the suburban, New Jerseyan land of my people. This proximity to my parents was always the safety net about which I never spoke, but always, *always* knew I had.

I thus shocked myself and everyone around me in 2010 when I agreed to go with a Non-Governmental Organization on a volunteer trip to Uganda. Seriously: Uganda. It all started with a random guest on my radio show who was doing humanitarian work in Uganda. The conversation went like this:

RANDOM GUEST: I'm doing humanitarian work in Uganda.
KEN: I would love to go to Uganda.
RANDOM GUEST: Then you'll come with me when I head back there in a month.
KEN: Okay!

And that was it. This trip to Uganda was my first *real* adventure and it fundamentally changed the way I approached the world around me. After chronicling the significance-laden, comical mishaps of my Ugandan journey every single evening in my journal, I knew for certain that the adventure bug had inflamed my meaning-craving addiction and I needed another fix. This was it! I had found an elusive sense of purpose and I felt really and truly buoyed.

And right then, with everything starting to look all rosy, my life just fell apart. Because that's the way it happens sometimes, right? My marriage disintegrated. My lifelong career evaporated. My deeply entrenched geographic roots disappeared. I was the very definition of "adrift," desperate for any anchor I could identify.

Not knowing what else to do, I continued what I had started in Uganda and threw myself headfirst into more adventures. And I wrote about these adventures in the only way I knew how: with my snarky gay Jewish voice, the voice that could never quite understand what I was doing in the middle of an adventure, but was relentlessly searching for meaning nonetheless.

And oh, the places I went.

As a weekend gym-goer who doesn't do major physical challenges, I somehow pedaled 425 miles in five days from Montréal to Portland, Maine. As an ardent fan of structure and explicit meaning, I somehow stumbled into a hippie retreat in Big Sur, California, for a weeklong exploration of the heartbreak that had just felled me. As a homebody who had never traveled much, I somehow returned to rural Uganda two years after my initial adventure. As a gent who likes control over all that is before him, I somehow signed up for an eight-day backpacking adventure in the Colorado Rocky Mountains, struggling to stand with a colossal backpack strapped to my shoulders and a half-ton of emotional weight strapped to my heart that I was desperately hoping to walk off.

But while I found myself in these adventures physically, the process of finding myself emotionally and spiritually was far more fraught. The only place where I was able to find any remote sense of answers to all of my questions was in that space that existed between my pen and my paper.

The words before you come straight from the journals I kept during my adventures: what I actually scribed by hand each night of every adventure. What you will read is *not* me casting my mind back years later to recall my travels. Instead, you will bear witness to these events as they were happening. You will come along for the ride with me a few hours after this snarky gay Jew spoke at a Pentecostal church service in rural Uganda. You will ride sidesaddle with me as I pedal my first ever hundred-plus-mile ride, cursing all the way. And you will pass out shivering next to me mere seconds after I was stranded all by my lonesome in the middle of that ridiculous backpacking trek.

On the surface, yes, these entries are about the trails and travels that were set before me. But, this is not a recounting of the bullet points and time stamps of my itinerary. Instead, the words before you are a daily diagnosis, a deep-dive analysis, and a reflective verdict on me: my physical and emotional struggles, my path to figure out my own voice, and, ultimately, my quest to figure out what the hell I was doing on those crazy adventures.

I mean: rural Uganda. Seriously?! *So* not Club Med. Like, at all. The citizens of Uganda had never even heard "Hands Up" before. And believe me, I asked.

I wrote for so many different reasons. I wrote to calm myself at the end of each unfamiliar day. I wrote to try to find meaning in the overall journey. And somewhere in there, I wrote to communicate it all to someone else. I don't know who you are or what brings you to these changes, but I humbly invite you to travel along with me in the hopes that we can find that purpose of adventure together.

That Time I Went to Africa

(Uganda: June 18, 2010 – June 25, 2010)

Day 1

June 18, 2010

I think I had a life outside of airplanes once. I'm not entirely sure because the past few days have been nothing but my butt in various airplane seats. Still, I'm feeling reasonably certain that I had a life out of airplanes once. "Once" being sixty-five-and-a-half hours ago.

Sixty hours ago, I got off a plane at Bradley International Airport in Hartford, Connecticut, having finished one of the most fulfilling weeks of my life. I was volunteering with AIDS/LifeCycle, the bike ride from San Francisco to Los Angeles. Before you get needlessly impressed, please know that I didn't sit on a bike at any point, not even for the smallest fraction of a mile. For seven days, I served on the Gear & Tent team, a group that packed and unloaded thousands of fifty-plus-pound bags for the thousands of cyclists each day. Now, I'm not asserting that the Gear & Tent work was a harder task than what those heroic riders accomplished by pedaling 545 miles. I'm just asserting that my work was different (also, it was harder).

In addition to the work, there was the fellowship. Without question, it was difficult being away from my husband (legally: "co-signer on the domestic partner paperwork," but "husband" just sounds better), but, in exchange, I lived in a love bubble where you called everyone "Hon" and hugs were the universal currency that everyone exchanged. I had never in my life experienced a week of unity and joy to the extremes I encountered there on AIDS/LifeCycle.

I followed those seven days of volunteering with two days of unadulterated revelry at Los Angeles Pride. Somehow, even after living in or around New York City for my first thirty-three years, I have never attended the NYC Pride Festivities; I never went anywhere near them. I had this faux-modernist view that every day should be Pride, so I conducted a boycott that went unnoticed by media outlets, LGBT magazines, strangers, friends, and family.

It was foolish. Los Angeles Pride looked me right in the face, laughed, and bellowed, "See what you have been missing?" And what I had been missing was an overwhelming sense of community brought together by love, fellowship, and yes, pride.

But parties can't last forever. Neither my liver nor my reserves of energy allowed the revelry to continue indefinitely. So, after what felt like a diva snap of the fingers, it was suddenly time to head back to my home in Vermont. I felt just as fulfilled as I was exhausted.

Coming back was a nightmare: the traveling was fine; the emotions were completely raw. In an effort to avoid sorting through said emotions, I had convinced myself it was important to be at work the next morning. Which was silly. There really is no actual need for a Dean of Students at a small rural school in Southern Vermont during the summer months when moose outnumber students by a ratio of 42:1. I sat zombie-like in my office for two days in a complete stupor: my body may have sat at my desk but my mind and my heart were most definitely hanging out in California.

Then, sixty hours after my return east, I packed largely the same clothes (thoroughly disinfected) in the same blue duffel and did what everyone does to process pivotal life events: I drove four-and-a-half hours south to New Jersey to set off for Uganda.

Seriously: Uganda. Which apparently is in Africa.

This trip came about so randomly that I haven't obsessed over it much. On a Wednesday last month, Gloria Thomas, a humanitarian/philanthropist based in New Jersey, was a guest on my gay radio show. She had received several mentions in the national press due to an open letter she penned to President Obama exhorting him to take action on the "Kill the Gays" legislation being proposed in Uganda. As I interviewed her, she spoke so passionately about her work with impoverished youth at a school in Uganda. I then made a flippant comment—as I do—that I would love to go with her on her next trip. She immediately replied that I would most certainly be coming with her on her next trip. Her assertion left no room for any other alternative. On Thursday, I asked my college to sponsor my trip. And on Friday, I had an email in my inbox confirming that I now had plane tickets to travel to Uganda. Which apparently is in Africa.

The trip's placement right after AIDS/LifeCycle moved it even further down my list of priorities. Normally, a transatlantic flight would trigger a healthy dose of anxiety in me, particularly if you equate the word *healthy* with the words *debilitating* and *overwhelming*, which I usually did. But my California experience had occupied so much space in my mind that there was little to no room for this *healthy* dose of anxiety.

It only started getting real for me when I pulled into Gloria's driveway and saw my twelve tripmates for the first time. We exchanged brief pleasantries. My face was sporting quite the fake and forced smile. In my head, I was shouting, *These are not my people! My people are gay and are all decked out in crazy costumes as we dance on the back of a Budget rental truck in California. These people now standing in front of me seem straight and suburban. I bet they don't even own a costume for a "Catholic School Girl Day" theme! These are not my people!*

Out loud, all I could muster was, "Hi. Yes, Vermont! Nope, not in New Jersey. I know! No. I've never been. Nope, I've never been. Yes, this really will be an adventure. Yes, it apparently is indeed in Africa. I'm so excited to get to know you too!"

Thankfully, our awkward first meeting was brief. Within a few minutes, it was time to set out for the airport. All of us smooshed sardine-like into a stretch limo for a ride that was interminable: bumper-to-bumper traffic, sticky hot, and, oh! Did I not eat yet today? Smart. Real smart. What was supposed to be a twenty-minute drive took closer to two hours, which made for an auspicious start to this journey.

I had steeled myself for a nightmare of a security check, but this wasn't Gloria's first transatlantic rodeo. We sailed through the process. I was accosted more by security in the Los Angeles airport last week for an inappropriate t-shirt than our group of thirteen was for our twenty-six, fifty-plus-pound bags chock-full of randomness including a rototiller, hundreds of beanie babies, and three hundred boxes of chalk that were spilling out of their flimsy cardboard containers. I had thought having your bags covered in white powder in a New York City airport would surely result in a body cavity search. Not so when you have Gloria pushing you through the system.

The flight from New York to Amsterdam was uneventful, mostly consisting of me trying to wrap my head around why I was on a flight to Africa even as I tried to distance myself from my journey to California. I was actually feeling pretty good about separating the two trips until I got on the plane from Amsterdam to Entebbe, Uganda. A deliciously and distractingly muscular gent was situated one seat away from me. As I stared not-at-all-covertly at his biceps, I heard his mouth, a foot up from where I was staring, utter two words that instantly pricked up my ears: "AIDS/LifeCycle."

Wait . . . what? What did I just hear? Did that guy with those bulging biceps attached to those broad shoulders connected to that—no! Focus, Ken! Did that guy just say, "AIDS/LifeCycle?" I couldn't help but leap headfirst into his conversation.

MUSCULAR GENT: . . . And that's why I couldn't do AIDS/LifeCycle this year.
KEN: Wait! I actually just got back from AIDS/LifeCycle!
MUSCULAR GENT: Really? I was signed up to be a Roadie.
KEN: Wait! I was a Roadie!
MUSCULAR GENT: Really? I was supposed to work with the Gear & Tent crew.
KEN: Wait! I worked with the Gear & Tent crew!
MUSCULAR GENT: Really? I worked with the Gear & Tent crew last year!

We immediately launched into a mind-meld sharing all of the people we knew in common, which turned out to be a pretty darn long list. He then pulled out his phone and showed me a text message that he received about me going to Uganda sent by one of my fellow Roadies with whom Muscular Gent shared a truck last year.

Quick reminder: I'm not on a plane from Los Angeles to San Francisco. I'm on a flight from Amsterdam to Uganda. And the deliciously and distractingly muscular gent one seat away from me has a text message on his phone. About me. Sure, it's a small world after all, but this felt all kinds of nutty.

I don't remember a ton about the rest of our journey even these few hours later. There were planes. There was luggage retrieval. There were packed vans. There was pure group-travel-exhaustion mode. I took the plunge and downed a few Advil PMs so I'm not sure how much time I have left to write as I sit here by myself in a hotel room in Entebbe, Uganda. Which apparently is in Africa.

My tripmates were all, "Oh my god, we're in Africa!" and, "Look! We're in Africa!" I'm just not in that awestruck headspace yet. I feel like a thing apart from their wonder, their amazement, and from the group itself. I was informed at dinner that we're traveling to the Equator tomorrow, so I'm sure the reality of being in Africa will start to hit then.

My biggest fears right now are that (1) I'm not yet in an optimal headspace for this trip, and (2) that the Advil PMs will kick in mid-sentence. Regarding (1), I keep thinking that *keep an open mind* and *be open to new experiences* are great mantras. But I also believe that your approach will doubtlessly be informed by the experience you've had, which, in my case, was only a few days ago in California. Ultimately, I need to be okay with (1) because (2) is muscling its way to the forefront of my life. As the chemicals are ushering me from being awake to falling asleep, all I can really comprehend is that there is surely an adventure in front of me.

◆———◆———◆

Day 2
June 19, 2010

Dear Makers of Advil PM,
Your product works.
With much appreciation,
Ken

I woke up groggy this morning. Turns out, jet lag is a real thing. I lay in bed for a few minutes until it suddenly occurred to me that I was in Uganda, so I quickly roused myself to start my first full day in Africa.

Gloria was the only other tripmate downstairs when I arrived. She pointed me toward the buffet and told me to get started. I loaded up my plate with various pieces of fruit and returned to the table and sat across from Gloria. She looked at my plate and told me that the pineapple would blow my mind.

I smiled even as I thought, *I promise you: no pineapple will ever blow my mind.* Then I ate the pineapple.

It blew my mind.

After thirty minutes or so, our group of thirteen assembled and piled into our van. As soon as the door closed, a few seconds before everyone was fully seated, the van lurched into motion and we were driving through the countryside. Only, it felt more like hurtling than driving. Traffic laws seem to be different here, in a nonexistent sort of way.

About six minutes into our journey, someone spotted a rainbow over the hills to our left. This wasn't some vaguely discernible suggestion of a rainbow. This wasn't some homage to a rainbow. This was a banded, each-color-distinct rainbow. Any trace of grogginess I was sporting instantly dissipated. It was an amazing promise of things to come.

The rest of the day was spent being an American and, at least for me, being embarrassed by it. Our van provided a cocoon that insulated us thirteen Americans from Uganda, a disconnect that allowed my tripmates to marvel at poverty while always maintaining some distance. But windows being transparent as they are wont to be, this meant that people could see into our van as well. We thirteen Americans, with our whiteness, our exuberance, and our pointing, well, we looked out of place to anyone who even glanced in our direction.

My gut reaction was to assume a veneer of self-effacement, apologetic at the intrusion that was so clearly a temporary arrangement, one that passengers and pedestrians alike all knew. We were not humanitarians moving to a foreign land. We were more like vacationers who would be volunteering a little bit. The thought of exclaiming, waving, and pointing—as everyone in the van seemed to be doing—well, that made me more than a bit queasy.

No matter what actual words my tripmates used in their excited utterances, all I heard was, "Look! You! You're exotic! You're exotic because I say you're exotic. And because I say you're exotic, I will take a picture of you to show everyone on Facebook that (1) you're exotic, and (2) that I accessed you."

I was suddenly struggling to follow my own thoughts. My head was a mess of cultural anthropology, sociological jingoism, and other concepts that I had never mastered but was still referencing. So, as I sat on that van hurtling through the countryside watching my tripmates exclaiming, I went internal and just plain clammed-up. Others in the van more than made up for my silence. I was feeling obnoxiously superior as I kept thinking that there should be a required "How Not to Be an Obnoxious American" course that every U.S. traveler should have to take (and pass) before they use their passport.

The Equator was a mix of heat (shocking!) and small crafty shops. We walked into a stationary-type store with handcrafted journals. The proprietor greeted us quietly. I said hello back quietly. The proprietor then greeted a tripmate behind me quietly. The tripmate behind me said hello back quietly. Then a third member of our group barreled into the store. The proprietor greeted him quietly. He bellowed hello and could not have been more au piercing to the calm of the shop.

In that shop, I quickly learned that you're supposed to haggle over prices. I also quickly learned that haggling is really not my thing. Turns out, I like the part where there is a price listed on items and then you go to the register and pay said price listed on said items. The concept of having to exchange words to mutually agree on a price made my anxiety shoot right up. So I didn't stay in that store for very long.

About thirty minutes after sitting around a café at the Equator, a small boy (maybe two years old), came over to where a tripmate and I, chips and homemade guacamole in front of us, were seated opposite one another in lounge chairs. The small boy looked at me. Then he looked at the chips. My tripmate offered him a chip. He turned to face her and then took a chip in his tiny hands. As he was carefully nibbling the chip, he continued facing my tripmate and began to back up slowly so that his back was against my knees. He stayed there leaning against me for a few minutes and soon—and I feel we did this in partnership—he was on my lap. The proprietor of the café came out to take some pictures of the boy in my lap as, apparently, he doesn't usually go anywhere near strangers. For my part, I was barely looking at him. For the boy's part, he never turned around to face me. He knew he was in my lap. I knew he was in my lap. It felt oddly natural and there really wasn't anything to talk about.

On the other side of the interaction spectrum, one of my tripmates was handing out pink Peeps—yes, those sugar-frosted marshmallow Easter thingies—to a group of children, but only after they were able to chant his name ("Frank! Frank! Frank!") and then successfully recreate his battle cry ("Let's go Mets! Let's go Mets!"). I fully acknowledge that my obnoxious anthropological superiority was again rearing its head, but I couldn't seem to help it.

Gloria soon informed us it was time to leave the Equator. The little boy hopped off my lap and sauntered away with nary a backwards glance or word of farewell thrown in my direction. Our group loaded into our van and headed off to Otuzzi, a remote co-op of a village that can only be reached by imperiling our van and its thirteen passengers on an insane dirt suggestion of a road. I was white-knuckling the seat in front of me the entire time, as it felt like our van could flip over at any second. This was most certainly a road-less-traveled, at least by van.

Upon arrival, we were immediately led into Otuzzi's Craft Store, the proceeds from which directly support the community. Eight craftswomen of Otuzzi sat outside while we shopped. The craftswomen often peeked in the windows to see which of their crafts were grabbing our attention. Our group cleaned them out. I bought probably $120.00 worth of crafts for around $10.00, and the villagers were apologizing to *me* about the high prices. I was certainly uncomfortable with their reaction but I wasn't quite sure how to respond other than to say, "Thank you." So I just said, "Thank you."

We also got a tour of Otuzzi's medical facility and their dentist's office. In the latter, there was a patched-together dentist's chair. That chair looked like it could fall apart during the next root canal. They don't have electricity, so a fancy, motorized one would be useless. But how about just a nice manual chair? I somehow got it into my head that this dentist's chair was my mission in life. I hadn't been in Africa for twenty-four hours, but clearly my purpose on this planet was to get the village of Otuzzi a new dentist's chair.

I began composing an email to the makers of dentist's chairs that would surely move a compassionate executive to immediately comp the village of Otuzzi a dentist's chair. But it wasn't enough for that compassionate executive to give it to Otuzzi for free, he'd also pay for the shipping and handling and have someone on site to install it. I had no doubt that Oprah would hear about my efforts and show up herself to put a scented candle under the chair for the first patient to discover. I couldn't believe it: I was going to meet Oprah! It was going to be one of the most satisfying hugs that I would ever experience in my life and not an hour would go by before she anoints me as her heir apparent. And to think, it all started because I saw a run-down dentist's chair and had a vision to make things better.

Obnoxious anthropological superiority and white privilege do funny things to the mind in a dentist's office in Uganda.

Day 3
June 20, 2010

Hey, remember that time when I sat through a three-and-a-half-hour Pentecostal church service in Uganda? Fairly sure I will never again in my life write such a sentence, so I tried my darnedest to be as present as I possibly could straightaway this morning. We were told next to nothing about what this church service would be like except that it was a three-and-a-half-hour Pentecostal church service. That description alone made me feel dreadfully out of place so my sole goal was to be in the moment. I was determined to not let that pesky gay Jew part of me interfere. Although I largely failed in this task, I would argue that there were a few moments today when I felt like I was there.

After a quick breakfast and a quick confirmation that yesterday's pineapple was no agricultural fluke, we piled into our van and drove to a hollowed-out suggestion of a church. Our group was immediately escorted to a few rows of white plastic lawn furniture set up front and center. Those white plastic lawn chairs were virtual thrones compared to the crude benches underneath the rest of the congregants.

This is not to imply that we sat much. Because we didn't. The service was nothing short of a musical revue: singing, dancing, clapping, praying, and pentecosting. I was mesmerized by the humans around me, and I constantly marveled at the movements of the churchgoers as I watched their hips do things my hips are not wont to do.

And suddenly I couldn't help but think about my father, Barry Mitchell Schneck. Barry is a man who has a relationship with religion, a bond with faith, a connection with the idea, structure, and culture of Judaism.

Have you ever been to a Bar or Bat Mitzvah? You know that guy who politely but sternly shushes the tween friends of the Bar/Bat Mitzvah honoree? These kids can't possibly understand the significance of the hours-long proceedings because the prayers and songs are in another language so they naturally start chattering away. My dad is the guy who shushes tweens into reverence and respect of the babel.

Barry Mitchell Schneck is faithfully present in temple every Saturday and I know that he derives comfort and stability from Judaism. It is firmly rooted in his core. The closest I have ever come to deriving comfort and stability from faith is my devotion to the pantheon of programming on the Bravo network. Although all those Real Housewives are firmly rooted in *my* core, it just doesn't feel like the same depth of reverence that my father embodies. I have often wondered what this relationship with religion actually *does* for my father and what I was lacking without it. It has always been a source of envy even as I have never made a move toward religion that wasn't mandated by my childhood dependent status on my parents. And even then, I attended services begrudgingly with a sour expression never far from my face (if it wasn't already plastered there to begin with).

In that Pentecostal service this morning, my mind tried to draw parallels between Saturday morning services at Temple Emanuel in Woodcliff Lake, New Jersey, and the one here in Uganda. Other than that they were both faith adjacent, this line of thought was like comparing apples to banana bread. For me, Jewish services are mostly staid affairs. If there was wonder and envy to be found in Temple Emanuel, I had to dig real doggone deep to find it. In today's Pentecostal service in rural Uganda? No such shovels necessary.

There was a fervency that was right on the surface of the entire church this morning. It was palpable. If I had been envious of my father's connection to devotion, this morning there I was feeling white-hot jealous. Throughout the service, there were two four-year olds in the aisle next to me alternating between dancing exuberantly and kneeling on the ground, scrunching up their faces, eyes tightly shut, mouthing prayers to above. Their whole behavior screamed of beseeching. I'm not sure for what a four-year old actually beseeches, but there was all kinds of beseeching.

The sermon provided by the pastor was an out-and-out doozy. It was centered on the power of voice. How do you use your voice? How can you make people hear? How do you vocalize the word of God and follow in the footsteps of Jesus Christ? Other than that last question, it all somehow hit home and took root somewhere in me.

Hilarity ensued when Gloria was called up to the podium and then called us Americans up one by one, handed us the microphone, and told us to address the congregants. Gloria, of course, gave us absolutely no forewarning that this was going to happen. There was no mention made over mind-blowing pineapple that we would be standing and making some sort of address to the congregants in a Pentecostal church in rural Uganda.

The crap that came out of my mouth about my heart being more full in my two days here than it has ever been before in my life was crowd-pleasing, even if I felt no conviction behind it. I know how to work a room, and this felt like the right thing to say. I got a smattering of applause and I was okay with that.

The tripmate who was handed the microphone after me sidled up next to me on stage and whispered, "You're an asshole for making me follow that." I shrugged.

There were more prayers, more singing, more dancing, and, yes, more beseeching. And then, just like that, it was over. It didn't swell to some liturgical climax. There was no eleven o'clock number. It was just over. And we were ushered from the white plastic lawn furniture back to our van.

The church is around the corner from Busingye School, our other destination for the day and the main focus of our entire trip to Uganda. As it is Sunday, the only students who were milling about were the boarders. And the only students who are boarders are orphans. When your main exposure to orphans is Pepper pushing Annie around in that laundry cart, Busingye on a Sunday is bound to be at least a tab bit eye-opening. And "eye-opening" doesn't begin to cover it.

There was one point this afternoon when I was crouched down next to a three-year old who was carefully tearing apart a large leaf into smaller components. I tried to distract him by poking his arm with a flower stem but he was not to be deterred. At no point did he look at me or acknowledge me, but as I was casting a shadow across him, and I was maybe four centimeters away from him, my guess was that he knew I was there. But he kept right on tearing. Could this have happened with any child? Sure. But I couldn't help but attach a different set of meanings to the leaf tearing given that he was an orphan. I transformed the scene into a giant metaphor because to do otherwise would be to be comfortable with the unfamiliar. Orphans in Uganda were unfamiliar and I couldn't have that level of comfort with them yet.

After lunch, I gravitated away from the group and toward the library to sit with Irene, the sister of the headmaster. She was dressed in a stunning orange wrap dress and a matching head-wrap. You couldn't help but notice her in church this morning as she led the children's choir. I later learned that her father is the Pentecostal pastor who had delivered the sermon on the power of voice.

Irene and I talked about American education and Irene began telling me of her own school that she opened on February second. I made her tell me the exact date because I knew that she knew the date. She brightened when she said that date. With fifty-four students and a huge chunk of them orphans, her needs were plentiful. She showed me pictures. I, in turn, melted.

I had purchased the three hundred boxes of chalk for the Busingye School and asked her if she needed any. She lit up. So I grabbed a whopping four boxes from the Busingye stash because that's all that were near me at the time. I gave them to Irene. No sooner did this chalk transaction go down than Joseph, her brother and the Busingye headmaster, walked in. His resting-face countenance was already stern and when he saw the chalk leave my hands and enter Irene's hands, the sternness in his countenance deepened. He looked at me as if I had given away one of his kidneys. It was uncomfortable and I bowed my head.

An hour later, in the van, Gloria laid into me, chastising me in front of all of my American tripmates. She was curt. Her words were clipped. She explained that Irene is a beggar and that it wasn't my place to get involved, especially as I couldn't possibly understand the dynamics of the situation given my limited time in Uganda. It was an epic dressing down of Ken and everybody in the van most certainly knew it, including Ken. My head immediately returned to the bowed position it had so recently left. It also gave me my first glimpse of Gloria. I had a sense she was not a woman you wanted to mess with. That sense solidified here.

Me being me, I couldn't stop thinking about this interaction for the rest of the day. The more I thought about it, the angrier I became. Irene started a school. She showed me pictures. She hadn't asked for anything. I bought the chalk with money out of my own pocket. Could I have been the victim of some long, well-thought-out, stunningly-draped-in-orange con? Maybe. But there were 296 boxes of chalk left for the teachers at Busingye School, four boxes for Irene's school, one headmaster with a missing kidney, one Gloria who dressed me down, and one bewildered gay Jew.

So, everybody wins.

Day 4
June 21, 2010

At the start of this day, I was determined to begin this entry with a dreadfully amusing witticism about feeling like a missionary, because our whole group wore matching beige polo shirts today displaying the logo of Gloria's nonprofit organization. Wearing matching beige polo shirts encompasses pretty much the totality of what I know about missionaries.

I was the first to arrive in the hotel lobby and had a few minutes to contemplate why the pineapple tasted slightly less sweet, which I attributed to my sour exchange with Gloria in the van yesterday. Then, as beige polo shirt after beige polo shirt arrived in the lobby, I started composing my paean to missionaries. Although I seem to have started with a reference to that dreadfully amusing parable, I have not and will not give it its full due because to do so would make me a complete tool given what went down today.

Today was our first full day at Busingye School and it was mind-blowing in a way that the taste of produce could never hope to match. Our van pulled up to the school's gate and we were all instantly overwhelmed by the sight of over a thousand children choking the school's paths. They were clapping. They were dancing. They were generally looking beatific. The reception was for us, a group that would henceforth be called "Our Dear American Visitors" by this community, with the pronunciation of the word "visitors" always sound more like "vis-tors," two syllables instead of three.

There was no pretending this reception was for anyone other than us. We couldn't pull off false modesty (jokingly looking behind us to see if President Obama had arrived). We couldn't pull off a show of embarrassment ("No, really, it's all too much! You shouldn't have!"). We couldn't pull off anything other than propelling ourselves forward through the throngs, reaching out to touch the outstretched hands of over a thousand children with over a thousand beaming faces. It was a special breed of sublime.

We were then ushered to the front of the auditorium, which, back home in America, would likely be characterized as less of an auditorium and more of a foreclosed shell of a large ballroom. We were again seated in the white plastic lawn furniture, which I am now coming to understand are like thrones for visitors. An hour of singing and dancing followed, punctuated tragically in the middle by our group being called to the stage to sing "The Star Spangled Banner." The audience could only have assumed our rendition was a hastily thrown together homage to Roseanne Barr, as if that reference had any meaning for the thousand-plus Ugandan children smiling at every missed note.

One of the songs and many of the speeches were in honor of "Gran Gloria." The canon went like this: at some point during Gloria's first visit to Uganda, she educated the headmaster of the school on how he could derive revenue from a set of billboards in the local village. In return, he dubbed her "Gran Gloria." Gran, or Grandmother, is one of the highest honorifics that could be bestowed upon a fellow human being here in this locale. The children sang to "Gran Gloria" as other children would sing to Santa Claus.

Throughout the performances, my eyes were everywhere, trying to take it all in. But every time I looked away from the stage to my group, another tripmate gained a small child on their lap. I at no point saw how these transactions went down. I don't know if my colleagues beckoned to the children. I don't know if there was an exchange of currency, actual or emotional. I don't know if incantations were uttered. All I knew was that I was the only one without a child on his lap, and although I feigned a little jealousy, I was really was okay with my lap being the childless outlier.

The rest of the day was significant, if a bit blurry. I remember being really anxious to start my project for the day, to feel in some way useful, to attempt to do something other than be a "Dear American Visitor" on white plastic lawn furniture. And apparently, my usefulness on this Monday was to be found in the wonderful world of dental hygiene.

Two tripmates and I were tasked with visiting every class at the school to hand each individual student a tube of toothpaste, a plastic toothbrush, and a small Dixie cup which had been donated by dental-minded benefactors in southern New Jersey. This seemed like such a straightforward task that would not merit many lines in this journal. Not so, dental-philes. Not so. There was so much dental drama to document.

First, there was the appreciation. When the Assistant Principal introduced us to every class and explained that they would be receiving these travel-sized treasures, each class broke into applause. For dental hygiene! Students brandished their tooth-brushes aloft as if each had pulled Excalibur from the stone. They were once and future clean-toothed kings, one and all.

Then, there were the logistics. We walked into many classes where the teacher was not even present and had to be fetched by one of the students. I highlight this not to label the teacher a derelict, as they were off assisting another class. But we're talking about a class of thirty to forty nine-year olds sitting quietly doing their work without an adult present. I tried my best not to think, *If that were an American classroom* . . . . But seriously! If that were an American classroom . . . !

Finally, there was more appreciation. Each student curtsied, some with their knees to the floor while whispering a barely audible "thank you" for their travel-sized treasures. My gently assertive *"kale"* ("you're welcome" in Lugandan) didn't belong in that same exchange. The teacher explained that the children's appreciation was in small part for the teeth-cleaning items and in large part for the hands of "Our Dear American Visitors" who were delivering the items from the land of opportunity. Can we say "humbling," boys and girls? Yes. Yes we can.

I can't remember a part of my day, save for a short break, which didn't have me immersed in children. But, even so, there were a ton of different and textured interactions. On one side were the nonverbal communications: sitting with children on a wall near the playground as they sat on my lap, felt the hair on my arms, looked at my pale palms, and touched my earrings. These connections were always with the younger children, who oh-so-gently pushed others out of the way to jockey for a better tactile position. I walked around campus today with at least two (and usually exponentially more) children holding my hands. If there was some room for pause about holding hundreds of hands of children with whom I had no previous relationship, it is not a space I can recall.

On the other side of this communication continuum spectrum was an incredible conversation I had with six twelve-year olds toward the end of that first day while I had a six-year old on my lap and another six-year old on my arm. It was one of those, "Holy crap, I wish I had recorded this!" conversations because it had that distinctive element of the surreal.

The boys started by asking me if I knew "Obama." There was no first name. No appellation of title. Just Obama. After I affirmed that he was indeed my president, I launched into this whole biography of Michelle Obama and her passion for children and the food they ingest. I thought it was so important to highlight Michelle more than Barack even as I really had no clue why. Their lack of interest in all things First Lady validated my wayward direction.

They then told me in no uncertain terms that the President of Uganda is a bad man who steals land. These twelve-year olds declared that it is important that the people vote him out next year. As political conversations and the potential for youth involvement never fail to energize me, I made them promise me that they would vote when they were eighteen even as I have no clue what the voting age is in Uganda. With these words, I hereby testify before the Ugandan Board of Elections that I may have just instigated some legitimate voter fraud. Apologies.

After our political roundtable ran its course, I asked them about their plans when they graduate. They expressed that they all wanted to be doctors, except for the six-year old on my arm who wanted to be a farmer. I asked them what life is like for boarders. They asserted that orphans smile just as much as others. And

I asked then what they thought about snow (I couldn't shut up about snow). They looked at me blankly.

They had this crafty method of indicating that they had something to say by quietly, yet audibly, clearing their throat. It was as adorable and obvious as it was respectful and earnest. The twelve-year old to my immediate right used the patented throat-clearing method to perfection as I was waxing on about blizzards (seriously, I couldn't shut up about snow). He cleared his throat and when I gave him the floor, he asked me if it was true that when babies are born in America, they automatically have parents, money, and a home. Without hesitation, I answered that no, this was not true and that many children do not have parents, money, or a home.

"Orphans?" he asked.
"Yes," I replied.

He nodded with a pretty crappy poker face that read equal parts surprise and satisfaction. I had so many questions that I wanted to ask him in that moment. Where had he heard that about American children? Did it change his worldview now that he knew that there were orphans in America? How did he think the issue of global poverty could be solved on both a macro and micro scale? What did he *really* think about snow? But I kept quiet, opting instead to let the moment pass in favor of simply enjoying the company of this inquisitive group.

I made the group all promise me that we would convene our klatch again. There was so much more for us all to discuss. But even as they agreed, I knew that I had no way to hold them to that. I was also so wiped out at that point that I'm not even sure I could assemble them again even if I tried. But I do want my own little Dead-Poet's-Society-Reading-Lolita-in-Uganda group, so I'm counting on a bit of fate to bring us together again.

Day 5

June 22, 2010

Here's a parable to ponder: When the wise old man tells the young scamp that he is going to teach him to fish rather than hand over the much-wanted rainbow trout, does the old man then stick around to make sure the scamp is successful post-fishing lesson? And if the wise old man leaves, does he take satisfaction that he imparted the knowledge? Or, if he does stay, and the scamp's line comes up empty, does the wise old man shrug and say, "eh, I tried?"

This morning, immediately upon our arrival at Busingye School, the nursery class all gathered outside their room. Their toothbrushes, toothpaste, and cups were in hand, ready for their first tooth-brushing flashmob. It was right then that I decided I wanted to be the old man who leaves after the lesson with a sense of satisfaction in hand, lest I be the old man who sees the scamps drop their brushes in the dirt, pick them up, and keep right on brushing.

Eh, I tried.

As the sun was already a blazin', the order of our day was switched around and we promptly set off on foot for the village of Busingye that surrounds the school. I'm not sure I really understood the point of our walking tour. In terms of context, it was an extended reminder that the school is situated in a particularly downtrodden locale. But no more downtrodden than the hundreds of other villages our van has careened straight through. Being more up-close didn't make me feel that context any more acutely. In some ways, this neighborhood exposure was more problematic, as the relationship between this village and the walled-off school seemed nonexistent.

Our group was given specific instructions before we set out to actually ask people before we snapped their picture, which I appreciated. My hope was that no one was thinking, "But the polar bear in the Central Park Zoo doesn't have to give his permission before I snap his photo!" The fact that I'm scribing that logic here should suggest that I'm confident that this very thought ran through at least one of my tripmate's minds. Also, I know for a fact that this very logic went through one of my tripmate's minds, as one of them said that very thing. She was, of course, "joking."

As we walked through Busingye, cameras and informed consent forms at the ready, we acquired our usual coterie of children following us around. This was irksome on a few different levels. First, although I will take one of my well-traveled tripmates at her word that our presence is the utmost in exciting to these children, I could never shake the feeling that we were a disruption. I wasn't sure whether the disruption was a logistical one that interfered with their chores for the day or if it was more of an emotional disturbance, as we were a walking billboard for the promise of funds. Either way, we were a disruption.

Second, there was the part where it was 11 a.m. on a weekday and none of these children were in school. Our guide explained that an enormous percentage of children from most villages don't attend school. Education is not a prioritized value in the face of the actual labor that needs to be carried out to keep the village running. So on we walked, pied pipers to masses of youth following us back to the school gates of Busingye School where they knew they could go no further: walls separating hope and promise on the inside from reality on the outside.

Of particular note and intrigue in our walk through Busingye were the villagers who approached us to have their picture taken. They would stand erect, we would snap the shot, and then we would have to show them the resulting image. Our guide deconstructed this process by explaining that the villagers were essentially asserting, "Yes, I'm real. Take my picture. And show me that you have done so." It was there that I learned that my disposable camera was an insult to the entire process. So noted.

When we returned to the school, we were immediately put to work on our daily task. I was given a digital camera and instructed to take photos of the two hundred-plus boarders holding up nameplates with their Lugandan and English names printed neatly. These pictures are used to track the growth of the orphans (with regard to their physical health) and to send back to their American sponsors to personalize the dollar a day their benefactors are sending to support these orphans. In my happy place, the emphasis is far more on the former than the latter, but my happy place is a pretty much a two-foot by two-foot plot after our walk through the village. That plot got even smaller when I learned that each child was then given a Beanie Baby after I snapped their picture. For some reason, those Beanie Babies came to embody everything that was troublesome about this whole photographic process. For what were these children being rewarded? Or did the children not care because they were now the proud owners of a bona fide Beanie Baby?

The resemblance between those photos and mugshots was present in every click. I learned the Lugandan phrase for "Say Cheese" (*Gamba ffene*) that translates more into "Say Jackfruit." I tried real hard to get each and every child to smile. And then I would think, "Screw it, they're orphans. Most of them lost their parents due to AIDS-related complications. They don't have to smile." And then I would think, "Just because they are orphans doesn't mean they have no joy!" And then I would think something else and then think something else after that, all so I wouldn't have to be fully present as I was snapping two hundred mugshots of orphans in Uganda.

After snapping thirty or forty of the two hundred mugshots, I fell into a stupor. This just didn't feel right. I wondered what the children knew about their American benefactors who probably and proudly displayed their sponsored child's mugshot under a "Life Is Good" magnet up on their fridge. I wondered why the orphans were told they needed to have their picture taken when their non-boarder classmates did not. I wondered how they processed the gift of the Beanie Baby for their time in front of the camera. I wondered and wondered and wondered some more, all so I wouldn't have to be fully present as I was snapping two hundred mugshots of orphans in Uganda.

After my experience as a photographic warden had concluded for the day, I was able to wander around campus as I pleased. I learned that I shouldn't walk too close to a classroom because the children had been taught to stop whatever it was that they were doing to stand and say, "You are welcome here, Our Dear American Visitors." It was as flattering to me as it was disruptive to their education.

There were so many other random moments of the day that stood out. At one point, I watched Nurse Liana sew up a gash on a child's head with a needle and thread. The child sat there stoic and prepossessed. Nurse Liana informed me that it is considered ill-mannered to cry out when there is a needle sewing thread into your head, even if you are a six-year old. I was in a daze as I helped wash the blood off the girl's undergarments, trying not to cry out myself. I was trying my hardest not to be ill-mannered.

Later in the day, there was an impromptu concert of celebration and appreciation that was convened when and because I approached a large group. It was a song that seemingly had no end and I eventually learned that my yelling "Yay!" and clapping only served to prolong the tune. Unfortunately, it took me eight full cycles of the song to discover that I was the root cause of the mind-numbing endlessness. Again, so noted.

But mostly, this was another day of my never having an empty hand. I'm not just fixated on the alien thing, the surface-level "I want to wave and stare and be near the strange man with the earrings" sentiment that these children seem to express. There is an affection to the constant attempts of the children to hold my hand. The thought of returning to a climate where a child cannot simply run and grab onto a stranger's hand makes me just plain sad.

Day 6
June 23, 2010

"Is she sick?" I asked Nurse Liana in near disastrous Lugandan. "Malaria," she shrugged.

Pre-Uganda, I had not thought to pair malaria with a shrug. I had thought a more appropriate combination would be to pair malaria with a gasp. Or to pair a shrug with the phrase, "It's raining again." But here, with a different context, new linguistic pairings emerge. This was the interaction that started my day and it certainly set the tone.

I spent a chunk of this morning with three tripmates and the headmaster of the school, traveling to a few of the secondary schools to take pictures of orphans who had moved on to higher levels of education. Apart from the first school being situated at the end of a vague suggestion of a road that I can't believe we actually drove over, it was a largely uneventful outing. I wanted to get through it as quickly as possible, as my feeling that our presence was disruptive had reached near-record level peaks. What little relationship I felt like I had at Busingye School was completely absent with these secondary schools. So it was essentially our group pulling kids out of class to take their mugshot and give them a Beanie Baby in exchange for their valuable time away from the classroom.

When the group had to set out again after lunch, I begged off explaining that we didn't need four people to take a picture. It's possible that I missed some big revelation out on the road, but I traded that possibility in for an opportunity to sit in on an actual instructional class at Busingye School. This was one of the best decisions I have made in recent memory. The class I chose to attend was English, taught in the P5 class, a group of more than thirty eleven- and twelve-year olds. Sitting in on this class should be required for all aspiring-to-be teachers. I was beyond riveted, more than a little bit humbled, and left feeling no small amount of awe.

As opposed to most middle and high school experiences in which the students move from class to class to spend time with a different teacher, here at Busingye School, it is the teacher who moves to meet the class. A few months back, I read a set of suggestions for improving American education that recommended this very change. It so clearly works. The transition from one subject to the next was not fraught with the logistical and energy-scattering issues of moving a large group of children through the electron collider of other groups of children engaged in the same frenetic movement. Unsurprisingly, it *is* easier to move one singular adult.

And then there was that one singular adult who stood before me for this class: *Musamesa* (Teacher) Gilbert.

Holy. Hell.

He was incredible.

Musamesa Gilbert strode in and immediately took firm control of the class. He had them stand and sing a song with various hand and body motions, immediately refocusing what very little energy may have been lost in switching teachers and subjects. I couldn't think of a time in my career that I had ever had a class so rapt so quickly. I settled in for what I knew would be an eye-opening master class in classroom instruction.

The topic for today's lesson was question tags: the fragment "isn't she?" in the sentence "Mary is going to school, isn't she?" With no books, the pedagogy was firmly rooted in learning by rote. *Musamesa* Gilbert was a constant blur of motion, moving swiftly up and down the aisles, gliding in between the desks, soaring up to the chalkboard (a cement wall covered with chalkboard paint), and just generally flying an inch above the packed dirt without kicking up even a mote of dust.

The students could not help but give him their complete attention, because to fail to do so would put you obviously and painfully out of synch with the verbal symphony that *Musamesa* Gilbert was conducting. Slouching, either in body or mind, was a sure and obvious way to fall behind. A stream of teaching from *Musamesa* Gilbert went something like this:

> *Stand up.*
> *Sit down.*
> *Girls stand.*
> *Boys read number two.*
> *Girls sit.*
> *Boys stand.*
> *Peter read number two and fill in.*
> *Boys sit.*
> *Class give Peter clapping (the class clapped three times for Peter).*
> *Jessica stand.*
> *Jessica read number three and fill in.*
> *Class give Jessica flowers (the class mimicked picking flowers out of the ground and handed the bouquet to Jessica).*
> *Jessica sit down.*

The pace was rapid-fire and I had to resist the more-than-convincing instruction to do all that was being asked of my young classmates. At one point, the assistant headmaster popped his head in to ask for a show of hands of vegetarians for Friday's banquet. The exchange took maybe fourteen seconds with control flowing from *Musamesa* Gilbert to the assistant headmaster and then right back to *Musamesa* Gilbert. I've been in American classrooms where a twenty-second announcement on the speaker system disrupts the class for minutes at a time. Not so here. There was no squeaking; this was a well-oiled machine.

Toward the end of the lesson, *Musamesa* Gilbert stood in front of the class, paused, and took what I thought was his first intake of breath since he began his instruction. He asked, "Who does not understand?"

Not one student raised their hand which either indicated a comprehension rate of 100 percent or a paralyzing fear of being singled out. Regardless of their motivation, given the presented flawless success rate of no raised hands, *Musamesa* Gilbert issued one final instruction to the class.

"Give your teacher flowers."

And they did. The class mimicked picking flowers out of the ground and handed the bouquet to *Musamesa* Gilbert. They did it happily.

This was my favorite part of class, and, perhaps, my favorite moment of this trip to date. I was smiling, the students were smiling, and even *Musamesa* Gilbert cracked a grin. And why not? Why shouldn't the teacher ask that his students praise him? Why do we often sublimate the role of *teacher* as if the role of the instructor is not an integral part of the process of learning for which students should demonstrably show appreciation? I have zero doubt that it gave *Musamesa* Gilbert a boost even as I fear that, in an American context, it would be inappropriately mislabeled as hubris.

In American education, the feedback loop for K–12 teachers comes from administrators and parents. It doesn't come from the students. In *Musamesa* Gilbert's classroom, the students are not denied the opportunity to recognize their teacher. And this truly is an opportunity for the students: a chance to comprehend how knowledge is delivered, a pause to explore how you can express appreciation, and a moment to actually make their teacher smile.

The rest of the day was spent playing a lot of soccer in a pockmarked field, shooting a few assorted orphan mugshots, and a ton more hand-holding. But my heart wasn't in it. My heart was growing flowers for *Musamesa* Gilbert.

Day 7

June 24, 2010

Today was unbelievably painful. And it was the least physical day I have had thus far, so you get the idea what kind of pain I'm writing about here.

To understand my plight today, you would need the background info that I have been cultivating a bond with *Musawo* (Nurse) Liana. The nurse's office, an eight-foot by eight-foot space, is next to the library that serves as our group's home base for the week. Every morning when we arrive on campus, I greet her in Lugandan. She, in turn, bombards me with a string of salutations never failing to ask about my wife—I neither had the strength nor the fortitude to correct her—and when said imaginary wife and I would be expecting our first baby. Throughout the day, she teaches me useful Lugandan phrases like, *"Oli muganda wange?"* ("Are you my sister?"), *"Ofumbye nnyo"* ("Thank you for cooking") and, my favorite anthem, *"Otulo tunnuma"* ("I like sleeping"). I used that last phrase at every available opportunity. It was a silly non-sequitur that never failed to make the children laugh even as it always (always!) rang true. I really do like sleeping.

Musawo Liana and I speak every morning about the students' medical issues for the day and how she is going to approach treating them. As I watched fifteen seasons of television juggernaut *ER*, I felt like I had something to contribute here. I was transfixed by her medical ministrations. She actually asked me to help her with a bandage at one point and I suddenly realized that my watching fifteen seasons of *ER* did *not* qualify me to the medical license I had always believed it had conferred.

Musawo Liana is also the only Ugandan with whom I raised the "Kill the Gays" legislation still moving through the Ugandan political process. It took me a few days of getting up the nerve but I finally asked her about it shyly. She shyly paused. She then shyly offered forth that men loving men was "very bad" and this policy might be a "good idea." I not-so-shyly changed the topic.

41

With our bond in mind, I was a bit apprehensive when Gran Gloria informed me at dinner last night that I would be spending the day checking *Musawo* Liana's daily logs. The goal was to make sure that her day-to-day entries were being accurately transferred to the student's permanent medical records that were established by a visiting team of American doctors back in March. Before I arrived this morning, I decided to work on this task in a building across the playground from Liana's office, because I didn't want to insult her by so obviously making sure that she was doing her job. But when we arrived this morning, Gloria announced, "Now make sure that Liana is the one doing the writing. I don't want you doing it." This suddenly meant that Liana and I would be working together on the insulting task of so obviously making sure that she was doing her job.

I quickly amended my role from one of "Quality Control Coordinator" to one of "Supportive and Goofy Helper." I actually greeted her this morning by saying, "*Musawo* Liana! Gloria said I can use the day to help you with any medical transcriptions that need to be done, not that you need this goofy American's help, but just in case, I'm here for you!"

Liana definitely hesitated. I think it was my use of the word "goofy." There was no Lugandan translation for that one. Whereas she normally would have greeted me with that string of salutations, this morning she just slowly nodded. I almost wanted her to ask me about my fake wife and the children that would be birthed by my fake wife. Instead, Liana already seemed dejected.

Regardless, we set up shop in the library and she produced a huge stack of paper, representing four months of daily log entries. I started flipping through the stack and asked her whether there were any entries that she knew needed to be transferred to the students' permanent records. She gestured at the huge stack before us. Turns out, a whopping none of that information had been entered into the students' permanent medical records.

Not good.

She then produced six huge worn binders of the permanent medical records with a vague suggestion of a system of alphabetizing.

Really not good.

I then started going through the daily logs and consistently found entries of students' temperatures of 107.9 degrees Fahrenheit (y'know, death) that then dropped to 91.2 degrees Fahrenheit (pretty much death) in a span of a few hours. I didn't need to watch all fifteen seasons of television juggernaut *ER* to know that something was amiss here. Two or three seasons would have been convincing on this front.

Okay, this feels beyond not good.

And when I went to transfer this information into the students' permanent records, I found that around 30 percent of students didn't have a permanent record at all.

Yeah, this task flat-out sucks.

I tried to ask questions that didn't sound like, "Hey, do you know this all looks bad?" Without meaning to, each supportive question that I tried to ask led to one disappointing discovery after another. I attempted to keep a supportive look on my face, but it clearly wasn't that convincing because, at one point, Liana looked at me and said, "I know I am disappointing Gran Gloria."

For hours and hours, I tried to help, which was made difficult both by the dim daylight in the library (no electricity) and my frustration derived from my own anal retentiveness. I gave up on the task once. I quickly went back to it. Liana disappeared once. I gave up again. I later discovered her hiding out by the kitchen, which is geographically as far away from the library as you could possibly get on school grounds. I knew this cartographical fact because it was a longitude I was obviously trying to reach as well. I felt sheepish being over there. I assumed that Liana did as well. But then she cheerfully asked me, "Ken, how is my paperwork coming along?" Her tone bugged me and we broke up a little in my head.

I don't know the full story here but that hasn't stopped me from forming an opinion based on the snippets I've been able to glean from Gran Gloria. Apparently, Liana failed to give out medications yesterday to all of the students who visited the dentist two days ago. Apparently, Liana is very dismissive of one of her supervisors. Apparently, Liana is lazy and just doesn't do things she doesn't feel like doing. Gloria had a pages-long list that didn't really match up with what I had seen of Liana in my brief time here.

That last tidbit is the one on which I became fixated as being an unfair characterization. It just can't be as simple as Liana being lazy and not transferring her notes to the students' permanent records. This transcription is not a shared value, neither for *Musawo* Liana nor for the school. Of colossal significance was her citing Gran Gloria as the person she didn't want to disappoint. What about the headmaster? What about the school? And, donning my full Sally Struthers/drama queen voice, what about the children? Who gives a fuck about Gran Gloria? Sure, Gloria is a huge source of funding, but she's obviously not a part of the day-to-day operations of Busingye School.

At dinner tonight, Gloria told me that she and the headmaster are sitting down with Liana tomorrow to have a big come-to-Jesus meeting. It felt like Gloria wants Liana fired, and if that's true, that means Liana will be fired. I didn't quite know what to say. I wasn't sure why Gloria was telling me this information. It almost felt like Gran Gloria was challenging me, but I certainly didn't know enough to weigh in on this human resources matter. So I just sighed.

In other news, I watched some students march a cow across campus to a slaughterhouse so that it could serve as the meat for tomorrow's banquet.

Otulo tunnuma. I like sleeping.

Day 8
June 25, 2010

So, while the deliciously muscular gent one seat away from me on the flight from Amsterdam to Entebbe (remember him?) had a text message about me on his phone, the guy on the other side of me was also insanely attractive. He worked in the coffee business so I naturally called him Insanely Attractive Coffee Guy.

Some backstory: Gloria had been attempting to produce income that would supplant the need for her to maintain her consulting business to focus on her Ugandan nonnonprofit organization full time. As part of those efforts, she secured tons (literally) of Ugandan coffee beans, but she could not secure a way to get said beans to the United States. I knew this before I met Insanely Attractive Coffee Guy but I was just so overwhelmed by the "I'm going to Uganda!" part and the "This guy is insanely attractive" part that I failed to get his card. Gloria subsequently chastised me for not getting Insanely Attractive Coffee Guy's card. It had been a nagging pinprick in my mind all week that I didn't get Insanely Attractive Coffee Guy's card!

On this, our last morning at our hotel, who is sitting at the table next to us?

Insanely Attractive Coffee Guy!

And then I heard myself exclaim, "You're Insanely Attractive Coffee Guy!" My filter clearly had been switched to *off.*

"Um . . . yes?" he said, using that tone of voice one uses when they are accosted by a stranger with a vague reference to their industry and a flattering, not-at-all-subtle and a bit creepy commentary on their looks.

"Amazing!" I responded. "Hey, sorry in advance for what is about to happen. Hey, Gloria! C'mere! Gloria, meet Insanely Attractive Coffee Guy. Insanely Attractive Coffee Guy, this is Gloria."

And within four to six minutes, Insanely Attractive Coffee Guy had sketched out exactly what Gloria needed to do to export her beans and gave her all the appropriate launch codes. I was feeling pretty good about my middleman status. Although I have never been completely sure, I think that brokering deals is what my father does for a living, so I felt like I had finally been successful in the family business. Or maybe he sells insurance. Either way, I was still feeling pretty good.

This was our last morning at Busingye School, and that weighed heavily on me, both because it was our last day and because it was to be a day-long party. There's so much more I wanted to do. So many more questions to ask. I've barely learned anything. Celebrations have most certainly not been earned.

As our van pulled up to the school, Gloria pulled me aside and said, "Ken, I want you at the teacher's meeting with me. I value your feedback."

Hey! Education! I do that! Heck, I have a PhD in that! This is a skill I have and I was excited to use it. It was almost as if the thirty-five years of student debt repayment that loomed in front of me melted away in the face of the use of this knowledge. Almost.

Plus, the validation from Gloria was not something I had experienced yet on this trip. Our relationship all week had been extraordinarily difficult for me to decipher. The banter we had on my radio show a few months ago was gone. I half-anticipated that loss because that was Radio Ken interviewing Humanitarian Gloria. Those are different people from Real Ken and Real Gloria. In person, I found her to be a walking contradiction: gruff as she fulfilled needs, harsh as she saved lives, no-nonsense as she provided sustenance. It wasn't *my* approach to this work but this also wasn't *my* work. I was thus intrigued to see what she had to say to the teachers.

All of the teachers assembled in the dimly lit library as rain beat down on the tin roof in a somewhat ominous soundtrack. Gloria had been asked by the headmaster to speak with the teachers on the topic of responsibility. To be clear, this seventy-three-year old Italian grandmother from New Jersey, who visits the school for *maybe* 3 percent of the year, sitting in zero of the thousands of classes taught by these teachers, was to speak to thirty Ugandan teachers on the topic of responsibility. Well, heck, given that context, the only possible tack for Gloria to take would be one rooted in the utmost in deference, right? Surely a falling-over-backwards contortion of praise?

Right before she was about to start lauding the teachers, she whispered to me, "Let me know if you think I should add anything when I'm done."

I thus had no clue what to signal from the back row when she began, "I'm going to be nice and I'm going to be not so nice." Followed with "Some areas are A-plus and in other areas, you absolutely fail." Crowned with, "After watching you this week, it is my responsibility to tell you that, in some ways, you really let us down." The widening of my eyes proved not to be an effective signal to add in some deference and praise.

The two areas of critique about which Gloria spoke were the unbelievable disrepair of the children's uniforms and myriad examples of the teachers not attending to some of the children's health issues. These were most certainly issues that needed championing, but I kept screaming in my head, *Say it differently! Change your tone! Use other words! Say it differently!* Gloria, however, couldn't hear my internal screaming.

The headmaster then took the floor and I instantly became even more uncomfortable as he delivered a litany of thanks to Gran Gloria. He promised that our group of Americans would be blessed in heaven. He then encouraged the Ugandan teachers to be more American. This was tempered slightly by Gloria encouraging our American group to be more African, but somewhere in between the headmaster's and Gloria's exhortation I had completely shut down.

This happens to me. Not too often, but it happens. I get so overwhelmed with trying to figure things out that I just collapse internally. I pride myself on being able to think myself out of a pickle, but every now and then, I can't find that neon red exit sign. Right there in the library at Busingye School in Uganda in Africa, there was no electricity present to light my path—certainly not literally, but also not internally. I have been spending the past few days forming so many opinions: about Americans abroad, about systems that perpetuate poverty, and about Gran Gloria. But sitting there this morning, a huge new reality came into existence and washed right over me:

I have no idea what this is all about.

I have spent five days in this school and I have no idea what it is like when "Our Dear American Visitors" are not present. In her remarks, Gloria closed by saying, "I know what you're doing even when I'm not here." I thought that it was a silly, Santa-esque threat. But as my superiority and notions of cultural dissonance rose, I again was hit by that shift in my thinking:

I have no idea what this is all about.

Gloria's nonprofit organization is a game-changing source of income and the thought of losing it very likely *may* be enough to be more attentive to dresses without buttons and feet needing bandages. Suddenly a ton of contradictions started doing battle in my head: making a difference versus imposing a culture on a people, preserving individuality versus limiting aid. It was a war and I found myself retreating to the shores of safety where I accepted that I couldn't fully understand this situation given my limited exposure.

This was not allowed to be a protracted war in my head as Gloria pulled me aside immediately after the meeting and asked for feedback. And here's where—and I own this—I myself absolutely failed. I told her that her words most certainly struck "an effective tone." Seriously: an effective tone. I actually said that. I felt like I failed everyone in the world with that response.

Gloria asked if we could sit down in the upcoming months to work out a mission statement for the school. I acquiesced, but only on the condition that the keywords for the mission statement would be pulled from the hours of footage that three of my college-age tripmates had filmed of the teachers and staff of the school for a film class project (and no, consent forms were nowhere to be found for that project either). If anything, the words of the teachers and staff would provide solid footing to offer ideas rooted in relevant practice. Especially as I just kept thinking:

I have no idea what this is all about.

The afternoon began with a banquet, huge heaping bowls of rice topped with either a vegetarian peanut sauce or that smiling cow who bid us adieu eighteen hours before. I was put in charge of sodas, handing out over a thousand bottles of fizzy. Following lunch, we were told that we had two to three hours to sit around in the library until the final assembly. I really wasn't in a sitting around mood. With my new reality that I didn't really understand the complexities of this experience, all I knew for sure was that I needed more experience. There were only a few hours left to go, so I looked around to see what other experiences I could cram into this adventure.

I wandered around campus and heard a chorus of laughter from behind the Girl's Dormitory. My feet followed the mirth, and I stumbled upon a group of older girls washing the thousand-plus plastic bowls that had been used for the banquet. Without hesitation, I elbowed my way into the center of the group and got to washing alongside them. They took me in immediately.

I had chatted with this group throughout the week and they had taught me phrases like, *"Totegeera"* ("You are silly"), *"Kenanyo"* ("Ticklish"), and a refinement in pronunciation of *"Ofumbye nnyo"* ("Thank you for cooking"), with that last phrase always earning me an extra slice of the mind-blowing pineapple. Hunched over that huge plastic pail with cheap, blue soap in one hand and shredded brillo-type scrubbers in the other was really one of the highlights of my week. We talked about America and their desperate desire to go see the schools and the children. We gabbed about boys and how they never ever do the dishes. And they shared their dreams of wanting to be teachers, each and every one of them.

At one point, a boy walked by and I yelled at him to join in on the scrubbing. There were gasps. There was shock. But, most of all, there was a boy suddenly sprinting away from the crazy white man. The girls and I all cackled and shared quite a hearty laugh.

When we were finished, I offered up my hand for soapy high-fives all around. One of the girls said, "Yes! *Tulibaluganda!*" That word had more syllables than any of the other Lugandan words I had been taught all week, so it had to mean something special. So I yelled, "*Tulibaluganda!*" back at her and all the girls screamed and yelled "*Tulibaluganda!*" joyfully back at me.

They explained that "*Tulibaluganda*" meant that we are all brethren. It is a word that brings people together in unity, minimizes individual difference, and celebrates that which unites us. It was a word that I didn't even know I so desperately needed.

Finally, with my hands all pruny and blue-stained, we were informed that it was time for the closing ceremony that would say farewell to "Our Dear American Visitors." Mirroring our welcome ceremony a few days ago, this closing was full of singing, dancing, and gifts for the "blessed Americans." It was quite a spectacle and I was merrily clapping along.

Then the headmaster announced it was time for "Our Dear American Visitors" to be baptized and everyone cheered. I cheered too. And then I processed what he said. And after I processed what he said, I began to panic.

"*Wait. What?*" I thought with a healthy dose of fear. "*You're going to baptize a gay Jew from New Jersey? Surely I will burst into flame the minute the water touches my head. Exit, exit, where's the exit?*"

Upon seeing my face visibly changing from unadulterated joy to sheer panic in seconds, one of my tripmates—who had previously been baptized in Busingye School—told me not to worry. This baptism, she explained, did not involve dunking. Instead, the headmaster would give us an African name, an honorific that would reflect the personality we displayed all week. My panic suddenly turned to excitement and my newfound excitement shot through the roof. I suddenly knew that, without question, I was going to get a tattoo of this word, so it had better be a good one.

My name was the first called and I walked to the front of the auditorium and faced the thousands of smiling faces. The headmaster bellowed, "Our dear Ken will be given the name of . . . *Mutebi.*" And the crowd went wild. I was beaming! I am *Mutebi*! I'll be getting the name *Mutebi* tattooed on my arm! My initials are KMS so maybe *Mutebi* was always present without me knowing it. I am *Mutebi*!

Also, what does *Mutebi* mean?

When I sat back down, I turned to the assistant headmaster seated next to me and said, "Psst . . . what does *Mutebi* mean?"

He replied, "*Mutebi* is of the *Mutebi* clan!"

"Great!" I replied. "But what does it mean?"

He explained, "Big, big honor. *Mutebi*!"

"Yes," I said. "And I'm honored. Truly. Thank you. But what does it mean?"

The assistant headmaster put his arms in front of him, flexed, and growled, "*Mutebi*!"

"Oh! I'm a warrior!" I exclaimed. "Is that right? I'm a warrior?"

The assistant headmaster put his arms in front of him, flexed, and growled, "*Mutebi*!"

"Um. A warrior?" I asked with some doubt creeping into my voice. "It looks like I'm a warrior. Am I a warrior?"

The assistant headmaster put his arms in front of him, flexed, and growled, "*Mutebi*! It means . . . Mad Fish!"

Mad.

Fish.

Here's a fun fact about me: if I have already decided on something without all of the information present, the rapidity with which I can justify my original decision before all of the information is on the table can truly reach the speed of light. I had already decided on the tattoo, so now that I was armed with the phrase "mad fish," I sat on that white plastic lawn furniture throne and rationalized my new African name posthaste.

Here's what I came up with in that moment:
1. Much like the darting mad fish, I, *Mutebi*, swim from issue to issue, task to task, in a social justice sea of interconnectedness.
2. Much like the tenacious mad fish, once I, *Mutebi*, sink my teeth into something, you have to filet me to wrest it from my grip.

After that, my rationalizing became distinctly more flimsy.
3. Everyone at Busingye School somehow knew I was a Pisces.
4. Maybe this was the adult ADHD diagnosis I always thought I sported but heretofore had never officially been given.
5. They appreciated the depth of my sole. That's right: sole.

Or maybe I didn't need to know what they sensed and could simply go with it. I should just sound my war cry wherever and whenever I can: I am *Mutebi*! Hear me roar! Sure, the roaring takes place underwater, where it just comes out as bubbles, but it is known on sea and on land throughout the world as a fierce roar. Roar! Glub! Glub! Roar!

Barely fifteen minutes after my fish-naming, we were ushered back on the bus, leaving the school in a turnaround that was jarring and unsatisfying. It was a hellish six-hour drive to our next location from where we would be commencing a two-day posh safari about which *Mutebi* does not care a whit. Not one fish flake of a whit.

I understand that, conceptually, the safari is intended to provide a low-maintenance transition back to the United States. But I couldn't shake the feeling that my Uganda experience, the one I came here to have, is at an end. I'm not sure what to do with any of it yet, which means I need more time to either figure it all out or to keep saying, "I'm not sure what to do with any of it," until the urgency fades and I swim on to my next venture.

I know that I'm appreciative. I know that I'm disoriented. I know that I am frustrated. I know that I didn't ask the questions that I wanted to ask and got answers to questions I didn't know that I had. In the back of my mind, I keep thinking, *I need to come back here* even as I have no clue how such a thing could possibly come to pass.

But, above all else, I know that there are answers to be found in *Tulibaluganda*. Somewhere in there is the key to unpacking the layers of appreciation, disorientation, and frustration. I need to figure out what I can do to embody *Tulibaluganda* in my daily life, to let it guide more of my thinking, and to somehow pass it on to others in my own mad-fish, *Mutebi* way. Until I figure it out, I need to sound my war cry wherever and whenever I can.

Roar. Glub. Glub. Roar.

Swim on, *Mutebi*. Swim on.

Pedaling and Peddling

(Montréal to Portland, Maine:
August 8, 2011 – August 13, 2011)

Day 1
August 8, 2011

How, oh how do I end up in these absurd situations? Promises. Plus stubbornness. Yes, I think the equation is promises plus stubbornness. That is what leads me to places so unfamiliar where all I can do is pause and freak out. I think that if I really put in the time and effort, I could recognize a promise before I make it and the stubbornness before I embody it, but I'm usually too busy freaking out to put in that time and effort. And the location where I am currently freaking out is a hotel lobby in Montréal. But that geographical information is the final piece of information in an epic Summer of 2011 tale, a summer that will henceforth be heralded as, "The Blurry Summer." So let's back up a bit.

The Blurry Summer was supposed to be fulfilling. Instead, it ended up being crap. I didn't write any of the articles I set out to write as even a vague suggestion of productivity was nowhere to be found. My fitness goals looked downright inspiring when written down, but oh-so-unachievable when I actually laced up my sneakers.

And the bucket list dream of going to Dollywood? Well, that got checked off but it was a complete and utter letdown. Seriously, if you're going to be a Dolly Parton theme park—a genius idea, mind you—then go all out and brand everything that is nailed down with a reference to Dolly Parton. I wanted to see rides named after her songs, carnival games that shouted out her movies, and fine, sure, some sort of reference to her chest. Not that such a reference would titillate me, nor would it do anything to shake my stance as either an ardent feminist or an ardent gay guy. That said, it's Dollywood. Give me some sort of reference to those two assets that Dolly herself repeatedly references. But, no, all I got at Dollywood were some of her songs piped through the park, a second-rate cover band that took more breaks than they did sing, and a museum sporting some of her dresses. It wasn't enough. Again, Dollywood was a complete and utter letdown.

Oh, and not only was Dollywood a total disappointment, but my relationship of nine years ended up in ruins. As in never-to-be-rebuilt-because-the-earth-has-been-sown-with-salt ruins, not hey!-let's-go-to-the-Parthenon! ruins. I had pretty much everything in life riding on this relationship. It was a union into which I had invested 35 percent of my years on this planet, 90 percent of my financial resources, and a good 18 to 19 percent of my ethics. And now it was gone and everything was blurry. Indistinct.

To find a path out of the blurriness, I briefly sought the assistance of a therapist, something I had never in my life done before. I have always encouraged the people in my life to seek support through therapy. I just would never consider counseling for myself. Therapy was an alien process to me and to all proud Schnecks who came before me. That I was taking the step to seek support in this way was shocking and significant.

Actually, I had to seek the assistance of two therapists. Therapist #1 told me in our second session that she would be moving to Italy in a few weeks and wasn't that exciting and couldn't I be inspired by her chasing her dreams? But I didn't feel excited. I didn't feel inspired. I did, however, feel more than a bit annoyed that she didn't mention her year-in-the-planning move during our intake the week prior. So, I guess annoyance was better than blurry and indistinct. With this emotional advance in tow, I moved on to Therapist #2.

Therapist #2 was quality stuff. She asked some hard questions and didn't let me perform nearly all of my crowd-pleasing feats of escapism that I had up my sleeve. Instead, she made me articulate a promise to help make things a little less blurry. She felt that I needed something to latch onto, a concrete step toward action that I could both articulate and fulfill. This felt significant.

The promise I came up with went as follows (and take this in slowly): the next opportunity that I had to do something that I really wanted to do but previously refused to do because my ex-husband wanted me to do it, I would do it. Got that? I knew it wasn't healthy to avoid certain activities solely because my ex-husband wanted me to do them. I knew it during the relationship, and I knew it after the breakup. But that resistance had become so ingrained in my modus operandi that, even in the aftermath of the relationship, I actively denied myself adventure and opportunity for no good reason at all. The promise to which this therapist was having me commit represented an escape route from that cycle.

The three things that I had identified and that I had always wanted to do but refused to because my ex-husband wanted me to do them were:

1. Take a Bikram class.
2. Learn how to drive stick shift.
3. Ride my bike more, or at all.

Let's detour here and diagram the complicated relationship between Ken Schneck and promises. Here's the thing: I make promises really quickly and once my mind is made up, I don't waver. Sometimes, you won't even finish your offer before I have already decided if I am going to do it. You could say to me, "Ken do you want to . . . ?" and before you have even filled in the blank, I have decided if I'm going to do it. And if I have decided I'm going to do it, I am in it to win it. It doesn't matter what it is: "Ken, do you want to . . . go visit NYC?" or "Ken, do you want to . . . go visit your parents?" or "Ken, do you want to . . . get married?" If I like your tone and am particularly bored and restless that day, I'm likely to say, "Yes, I want to do that!" before you have finished making your pitch. And once I have set my mind to do it, I fucking do it.

Because I knew how I threw myself into promises and because I wasn't quite ready to change my modus operandi and do any of those three things on my promise list, I avoided those opportunities at all costs. Changes most certainly had to be made. I started by defriending everybody on Facebook who I knew had anything to do with yoga. Which, if we're being honest here, I had always kinda wanted to do anyway. I stopped riding in cars that I knew were operated by stick shift. Which, if we're being honest here, I don't even really accept is a thing. Attention stick shift drivers: they actually make cars where you don't have to constantly be doing all that shifting and clutching and stalling! You can just put your car into the gear you want, and it will go forward or backward depending on which direction you have specified that one time. Yes, you are great multitaskers, but you can relax on this one task.

But what I couldn't do, what I could never do, was avoid email. And when that one email came in with the subject line, "Come on our bike ride next week!" I knew I was caught. It was the fulfillment of promise #3 and that subject line jumped off the screen and landed in my heart. Before I even opened that email, I decided right then, "Yes. Yes, I will go on this bike ride next week." I had articulated, made, and cemented the promise.

And that's how I committed to pedaling Charity Treks: a five-day bike ride from Montréal, Canada, to Portland, Maine, to raise much-needed money to find a cure for HIV/AIDS.

425 miles.

But I promised!

In that moment, when I opened the email and realized the commitment I had made, I was remarkably lacking in any sense of worry. My sudden burst of confidence was derived from four main sources of rationalization:

Rationalization #1 — I had an amazing bike. A truly great road bike. Everyone who saw that bike sitting in the living room, unused, more than slightly dusty, and holding up a planter, commented, "Now that, that is an amazing bike."

Rationalization #2 — At the gym, I could rock out thirty-five minutes on the elliptical at level twelve with absolutely no problem. Surely this bike ride wouldn't be that strenuous. Seriously! Thirty-five minutes. On level twelve!

Rationalization #3 — I have an amazingly poor sense of cartography and topography. When I read that e-mail, I really and truly thought, "Hmm. Montréal to Portland, Maine. Canada to the United States. Canada is geographically above the United States. Hmm. Well, that sounds like downhill to me!" Let this also serves as another reminder that people with PhDs are not smart in all things.

Rationalization #4 — I suck at math. I mean I really and truly suck at math. It never has been my thing and likely never will be. If you read that email and saw, "425 miles over five days," what would you have come up with for the average daily mileage? <pause for you to shout out your answer> Yes, I see you and hear you and validate you and thank you for surfacing that answer. But what I had come up with was more like forty miles a day. And I was comfortable with both my calculation as well as my ability to pedal forty miles a day. Again, thirty-five minutes on the elliptical! At level twelve! Also, let this also serve as a reminder that people with PhDs are not smart in all things.

This being Blurry Summer and all, I didn't train much. There was that one time that I biked thirty-five miles. It was ok. My legs hurt the next day. So, I went back to level twelve on the elliptical machine. One day, I even jacked the elliptical up to level fourteen for three or four of those thirty-five minutes. I was feeling pretty diesel.

I bought some used biking jerseys online with logos emblazoned across the chest heralding the completion of rides I had never completed. If anything, I was going to look the part. I wore one of those jerseys on that one thirty-five-mile practice ride. Another cyclist I passed on the road pointed to my jersey and yelled, "You rock!" Yes, sir. I do rock. I do rock at shopping for used jerseys and I thank you for taking notice!

The summer flew by. Or maybe it didn't. I'm not really sure because it was blurry. Regardless, it was either suddenly or finally time to depart for Canada. I saw on the Charity Treks Facebook page that there were two riders living in my town in Vermont who needed a ride to Montréal. I offered them a lift and they happily accepted. We three met at one of their houses this morning and he highlighted that I didn't have a bike rack to which all three of our bikes could be attached to the rear of my car. Apparently, this was both an important detail as well as a detail that hadn't occurred to me. Thankfully, one of them had an extra bike rack and he attached it while they both looked at me a little funny. I smiled mightily back at them lest they think I was anything other than the hardcore cyclist that I obviously wasn't.

The drive up north (which, mind you, was uphill in my head) was pleasant and my two cyclist passengers recounted their many tales of bike rides across New England. I countered with tales of my many car rides across New England. I just kept on smiling mightily back at them lest they think I was anything other than the hardcore cyclist that I obvious wasn't.

For the majority of the car ride, I mostly stayed in my own head and focused on the music so that I didn't have to focus on the enormity of the journey in front of me. This enormity was most certainly starting to set in on the drive to start a bike ride for which I was starting to feel like maybe I wasn't 100 percent prepared. And by "maybe," I mean that I was in no way prepared for this journey.

And then I heard it.

A number was thrown out into the air by one of my passengers. It was a number that cut through all of my artificial rationalizations, delusions, and blurriness: 113.

KEN: Wait. What? Did someone say 113?
CYCLIST PASSENGER: <cheerily> Yes. 113.
KEN: 113 what, exactly?
CYCLIST PASSENGER: <cheerily> 113 miles.
KEN: Right. 113 miles.

<pause>

KEN: What were you saying about 113 miles?
CYCLIST PASSENGER: 113 miles. That's how much we are all
pedaling tomorrow on Day 1.
KEN: <laughs>

Really, all I could do was laugh. If you have read a single word up
until this point, then I don't need to take the time here to underscore the absurdity of 113 miles. But if I were to take the time to
underscore the absurdity of 113 miles, I might highlight that 113
miles is more than three times as far in distance as my singular
thirty-five-mile training ride. It took me a few minutes, but I actually did the math on that one. On a calculator.

For the rest of our journey, we talked about myriad topics.
Many of those topics had absolutely nothing to do with cycling.
But then, the concept of 113 miles would pop into my head and I
would start laughing. My passengers looked at me with more than
a bit of concern when these random bursts of laughter erupted,
which happened at least five times on the drive, and possibly more
than five.

Sensing that I was perhaps less than prepared, my passengers
tried to give me advice, but I wasn't able to process anything other
than the absurdity of 113 miles <cue Ken's laughter>. They spoke
often of "drafting," advising me not to try it for the first time on
the ride. That really wasn't going to be a problem for me because
I had no idea what drafting was and I refused to ask. Because,
y'know, 113 miles <cue Ken's laughter>.

When we finally arrived in Montréal, we checked into our
hotel and scattered: they to their room, me to mine. I had a
sense that my freaking out alone in my room was maybe not the
healthiest route to getting through the night. So now, instead,
I'm freaking out in a hotel lobby in Montréal, listening to front
desk clerks speaking in French. I don't know what they're saying, because I took Spanish in high school. Dan Cappello, the
valedictorian from my Pascack Hills High School Class of 1995,
well, he took French. He's gay now. With hindsight, he always

was; he was obsessed with Jackie O and *The Golden Girls*, but somehow I was the one whose car got spit on even though both of us were in the closet. Now he runs some sort of website for Manhattan socialites.

Tonight, I sat in a lobby of a hotel in Montréal and surfed Dan Cappello's website for Manhattan socialites for an hour. Although I wasn't able to discern its function, Dan's incredible writing distracted me from the thought of 113 miles. Or, at least, it distracted me enough so that I calmed down a slight bit, which is not to say that I was able to completely put a stop to all of the laughing.

Indeed, I laughed to myself for quite some time tonight. I think I scared the French receptionists; those looks transcended language barriers. I can't help but think I have no business being here, but here I sit. I made a promise and now I'm in it. I just need to somehow figure out how to win it.

Day 2
August 9, 2011

I'm going to ruin the ending of this entry: I pedaled every centimeter, every inch, every foot, and every yard of 113 miles today. I thought you should know that right upfront before I recapped the insanity of this day. Can you believe it? I can't. Particularly as things today did not start out well. At all.

Unsurprisingly, it was a pretty uneasy sleep last night: part anxiety, part someone snoring loudly in the room next door, part lack of both Ken's battered, Tempur-Pedic pillow as well as Ken's stuffed cow, named Cow.

This morning, I was just a panic-ridden mess. I thought the clips on my shoes were broken. They weren't. I thought my tires had enough air in them. They didn't. I thought not eating breakfast was an okay idea. It wasn't.

In order to calm myself, I did what I do to get through life: I went inside myself, I centered my chakras, and I harnessed my chi.

Okay, I didn't do a single one of those things because I don't do a single one of those things. But I did do the deflection thing that I have previously mastered and instead focused on other people.

I noticed right away that the demographic of the ride is different from the multiple AIDS-related bike rides I have worked in the past. There are only a handful of participants here who are under the age of forty, and most of the under-forty crowd are female. Young gay men are not the core audience here. In fact, it didn't look like gay men were the audience here at all. This tiny ride of seventy riders (as opposed to AIDS/LifeCycle, which boasts a roster of twenty-five hundred riders) seemed to be a lot of straight white men over the age of forty-five. My two passengers from yesterday were straight, white men over the age of forty-five, but I assumed that they would be in the minority on the ride. When I looked around this morning, I realized that *I* was the one in the minority.

I have attended a lot of Opening Ceremonies in the past and they never fail to be emotional affairs. The Opening Ceremonies on AIDS/LifeCycle feature a rider-less bike that symbolizes all of our brothers and sisters who we've lost in the epic struggle against this disease. This then transitions seamlessly into the riders setting off on their bikes, pedaling into the distance to combat and defeat the deadly foe of HIV/AIDS. This morning's Opening Ceremony was . . . um . . . not that. The two motivational speakers were two straight men, one of whom had a coworker whose brother was recently diagnosed with HIV. This ancillary tale didn't really motivate me to pedal. At all.

One highlight of the Opening Ceremonies was my finding two women with whom I was excited to ride alongside. Long ago, I was taught that fail-safe trick that, if you're feeling significantly less than confident, surrounding yourself with individuals who appear to be even more freaked out than you can ultimately help fortify your fragile state of being. Screw that "rising tide lifts all boats" crap; I really wanted to not feel like the most freaked-out person in Canada. These two young women's eyes seemed as wide as mine, so I sidled up next to them and asked whether we could ride together. They both smiled and nodded. I instantly knew I had my gaggle for the week ahead.

After the Opening Ceremonies had concluded, our group of three rode out with one of the last groups to leave the hotel parking lot. We pedaled through the streets of Montréal and I absolutely hated that first hour. We hit every red traffic light and it was then that I learned that apparently bicyclists are supposed to follow the same traffic rules as people in cars. Who knew? That very important rule wasn't in any of the materials I had failed to read before we set out (I later learned that this very important rule was indeed in all of the materials we had been sent). Hitting every possible traffic light was tremendously tedious. Red light after red light; clipping in and clipping out of my shoes. My hope was that I could Zen out and just pedal through my anxiety. The traffic laws of this civilized Canadian colony prevented that from happening.

My learning curve became even more steep when I realized there is a whole cycling lingo and a set of corresponding hand motions that you're supposed to know. I was never taught the cycling lingo or the set of corresponding hand motions there on the elliptical machine. If you're slowing, you apparently yell out "Slowing!" to those behind you with the palm of your hand held facing back toward traffic, other riders behind you, and out from the side of your body. If there is debris on your right, you apparently yell out "Debris right!" to the person behind you and point to it with a circular motion. And, if there is a car approaching, you apparently yell out, "Car back!" to those in front of you (no motion needed because those in front of you can't see you).

That last notification proved to be the most important for me as I was always in the back. I guess I didn't master the lingo right at the start this morning. It's not as if I wasn't trying to warn— and thus protect—the riders in front of me. I just thought that a lengthier exposition might be more helpful. My narrative sounded something like:

Hey folks! I just wanted to let everyone up there know that there is indeed a car coming up behind us. It has a bluish hue, maybe a Subaru of some sort, which demographically sounds right because we are indeed so close to Vermont and there sure are a ton of Subarus in Vermont. It's like the official Vermont state car. Anyway, yeah, he's coming up behind us and he does look a little bit angry but I can see that he has a pretty cool bracelet on so maybe he's not all that bad. So, yeah, car coming up from behind. Car back. Keep pedaling everyone. Go team!

At the next traffic light, one of the oldest female participants pedaled up next to me and greeted me so sweetly with a "Honey" salutation. She was adorable. She then said, "Really . . . fucking 'car back.' That's all you need to say." So sweet. So adorable.

More and more red lights appeared before us, creating more and more starting and stopping. Then, without warning, the traffic lights disappeared, and we were out of the city of Montréal. My two awesome women and I were untethered by traffic safety and things started going well. We pedaled. We pedaled a whole lot. There was even one point when I broke away from the pack and was flying down a highway in the rain by myself. I have passion! I have freedom! I have . . . a flat tire!

And it wasn't just a gradually deflating flat tire. I hit a pothole, and that tire exploded. When I mess up, I mess up dramatically. Turns out, I'm even a drama queen when it comes to flat tires. Three thoughts immediately flashed through my head: (1) *Fuck!*, (2) *I don't know how to change a flat!*, and (3) *Fuck!* Thankfully, this is a fully supported ride and a crew car stopped within forty-five seconds and offered to shuttle me to the next stop, as it had started raining pretty hard. But I resolutely wanted to pedal every mile; I had made a promise. So we fixed my tire right there in the rain. And by "we," I mean, "the guy in the crew car who actually knows how to fix a flat tire."

My tire-fixing knight was amazing. He was explaining everything that he was doing. He was doing this with the lever and that with new tube and something else with the pump. But, by far, the cutest part of all was when it suddenly clicked in my head that he was not only explaining what he was doing, but that he also thought I was listening and learning. Although I was physically present, all I heard during the process was the teacher in Charlie Brown. When my savior finished the repairs, he cheerily said, "Well, you are all set and now you will be able to fix your next flat!" I explained to him that, no, I really would not be able to do that. He was, thankfully, amused.

With my tire now filled with air, I just kept on pedaling. And then, many hours later, I was done. Just like that. Now, I'm a little dazed and somewhat embarrassed as, again, I really had no business biking 113 miles. But I'm done with Day 1, and I'm 113 miles closer to fulfilling this promise. That's definitely something and even more remarkable, I actually feel in my heart that it is something. Sure, I can't really feel my legs right now, but who needs feeling in their legs to pedal a bike?

Right?

* —————— * —————— *

Day 3
August 10, 2011

Fun fact that I learned today: ninety-seven miles can actually be astronomically more challenging than 113 miles. I had assumed that the bigger the number, the harder the ride. Turns out: no, that's actually not always the case.

I woke up sore, but when I willed my legs to move, they actually did so I was feeling pretty good about that. Small victories like your legs moving, y'know? After all, I had pedaled 113 insanely hilly miles, climbing and climbing and conquering every huge mountain ahead of me. Surely I could do ninety-seven miles with no problem.

During breakfast, I sat with an experienced rider who had been identified yesterday as a cyclist who had participated in every one of these rides since they were created a decade ago. After some small talk, we had this delightful exchange:

ACTUAL CYCLIST: How did you do yesterday?
KEN: I think I did really well. I pedaled every inch.
ACTUAL CYCLIST: Well done! Do you do centuries often?
KEN: I don't know what that means.
ACTUAL CYCLIST: Centuries.
KEN: You just used the same word. I still don't know what that means.
ACTUAL CYCLIST: Centuries are rides of a hundred or more miles.
KEN: Oh. Yes, that now makes sense as a word. No, yesterday was my first one.
ACTUAL CYCLIST: Your first century was yesterday?!
KEN: Yes.
ACTUAL CYCLIST: That's so great!
KEN: Yeah, I can't believe how I was able to get up those monster hills all day long!
ACTUAL CYCLIST: <laughs> Ha. Very funny!
KEN: Um . . . I wasn't trying to be funny.
ACTUAL CYCLIST: I just meant that the joke about the monster hills was funny.
KEN: That wasn't a joke.
ACTUAL CYCLIST: Um . . . you know that yesterday's route was pretty much flat, right?
KEN: No. No, I did not know that.
<end scene>

My two female companions and I set off with an earlier group and I was determined to stick with my amazing gaggle throughout the day. And then, at some point pretty darn early in the day, I ended up on my own and that's pretty much how the day went. I wasn't even sure how it happened, but there I was out on my own.

It didn't take long for me to discover that my breakfast companion's assessment of yesterday's topography was wholly accurate. It's almost like I didn't know what hills were until today. I pedaled up the hills alone. I coasted down the hills alone. The former felt like it outnumbered the latter by a good 6:1 margin. I will note that, as hard as hills are, I was infinitely more comfortable climbing them than speeding down them. Sure, climbing hills hurts and hurts bad, but I usually keep my head down, grit my teeth, and try to slog through it. Flying down the hills freaks me out; I end up gripping tightly on my brakes, as I want nothing more than to have control over my situation. Because I'm sure that's not a metaphor for something larger, right? Right.

There were many significant chapters in today's ninety-seven-page novel, and every significant bookmark had me feeling like an idiot as a result of my not knowing anything about bikes except how to pedal and, every now and then, to switch my gears. My brain has never been one to be able to grasp mechanical concepts. Add my profound propensity to avoid things I can't grasp to my existing mechanical deficiency, and you end up with my truly stunning lack of knowledge about this piece of metal on two wheels that has to get me through 312 more miles. What I don't avoid, however, is the opportunity to look pathetic and pleading when even the most minor mechanical failure mars my journey, which they did all the livelong day today.

My bike chain came off. I looked pathetic and pleading. Someone fixed it for me. I kept on pedaling.

The clips on one of my shoes broke off. I looked pathetic and pleading. Someone fixed it for me. I kept on pedaling.

My bike chain fell off again. Now there I got annoyed. I had it in my head that these things couldn't happen more than once. I saw it as some sort of checklist and, once you experience a biking malady, it wouldn't happen again. It just couldn't. But, there I was with a dangling bike chain. I looked pathetic and pleading. Someone fixed it for me. I kept on pedaling.

With all of the minutes spent pedaling by myself—and there were a lot over ninety-seven miles—there was a heck of a lot of time to do some thinking. I processed thoughts that existed on both a practical level as well as thoughts on a more emotional plane.

Regarding all things practical:
1. I drew my next tattoo in my head.
2. I planned what I thought would be a pretty cool fundraiser that I could throw when I returned to Vermont.
3. I confirmed, via a most successful run-through, that I could indeed step into any role in *Dreamgirls* at the last minute without missing a line or beat, be that performance Broadway or local.

On the emotional side:
1. I spent many, many miles mourning my failed relationship.
2. I devoted more than a few miles chastising myself for my own irresponsibility in not learning a thing about bike mechanics.
3. I marveled for three or four yards at what I was doing. At one point, I actually thought, *Hey! Look what you can do if you put your mind to it!*

That last thought came after a particularly brutal hill that I climbed and climbed, head down, determined to make it. When the ground leveled out, that thought rang out: *Hey! Look what you can do if you put your mind to it!* Anyone who knows me, has read my writing, or has even walked by me on the street, has likely concluded that I'll never get offered a job at Hallmark. That kind of schmaltz was most uncharacteristic.

But it really was a genuine thought, and for those three or four yards I really did believe it. As I finished today's ninety-seven hilly miles, I couldn't help but remember that moment and I smiled.

I ate a quick meal, set up my tent, and am about to pass out, all with that smile still lingering.

Day 4
August 11, 2011

Today flat-out knocked me down.

The journey was only fifty-nine miles, significantly fewer miles than the other days, but the hills were beyond insane. Each hill was the bottom of another hill, which then turned out to be an anthill, which was located at the base of an Everest. It was mile after mile of hills, the sun blazing down on a shimmering highway largely devoid of cars. There were no landmarks to distract the riders, just endless miles of concrete to slog through.

I could have latched onto many emotions to get through the day. For some reason, I chose anger. And pretty intense anger at that. I was furious, truly, at nothing. I kept thinking, *This is such bullshit!* as if someone had done this to me. I was transformed into a veritable cussing machine, which is very much not my normal baseline. I'm far from prim and proper but I generally don't cuss much, as evidenced by the fact that I use the word "cuss." This morning, however, cusswords started flying out of my mouth with reckless abandon. By lunch, I had largely calmed down, but holy hell was I seeing red this morning.

In inter-rider news, there was a little bit of drama today. It was rooted in the sparse bit of bike safety that I actually did know when I set out a few days ago. When you're out there on the road, it is so unbelievably important to yell out "On your left!" when you approach other riders to pass them. If you're pedaling mile after mile, you can really zone out and if someone just suddenly pops up next to you, it can be really and truly startling, a state that doesn't lend itself to safe and effective pedaling or balance.

For the past two-and-a-half days, there has been a group of three riders—two males and a female—who kept passing us without saying anything. These very fit, very athletic, very cyclist-looking riders would pop up suddenly and silently on our left, pass us, and arrive at the next pit stop ahead of us. My group of three—my two female companions and I—would arrive at the pit stop, quickly refill our water, eat some snacks, and set out on the road before the other riders because we knew we weren't as fast as everyone else and we didn't want to fall behind by the end of the day. Then, a little bit later, those very fit-looking riders would pop up suddenly and silently on our left, pass us, and the cycle began anew.

Our group was really annoyed by their group but the three of us were feeling extraordinarily nonconfrontational. Well, more specifically, we were feeling extraordinarily not-directly nonconfrontational; passive-aggressive behavior was fully within our grasp and we employed it creatively. We concocted a fully fleshed-out narrative where this bike trip was some sort of international competition. We labeled ourselves "Team USA," as we were feeling inexplicably but resolutely patriotic. We labeled the other group "Team Germany" because they always blow by us on the road without saying anything and, thus, were obviously fascist.

This narrative gave us great pleasure and truly even motivated Team USA through some particularly tough stretches of road. It wasn't a narrative that we shared with anyone else on the ride, but it was not uncommon to hear one of us yell something like, "No! Team Germany has taken the lead again! Come on, Team USA! Do it for the children. The American children!" Anyone who overheard us likely thought we had lost our marbles, but we giggled on, which was a far preferable state than my earlier state of extreme anger and cusswords.

When Team USA arrived at tonight's camp—we called it Olympic Village—there were only three seats left at one of the many six-person tables for those bringing up the rear. And the seats already taken at the table were occupied by—you guessed it—Team

Germany! After some initial awkward moments overcoming our respective language barriers, the conversation blossomed into one of the most beautiful displays of international unity that the world has ever seen.

Team Germany turned out to be lovely. We laughed together. We swapped silly jokes together. We shared heartfelt stories together. Team USA let slip that we assumed they were fascist. The six of us had the most grand time at that small table and we made a pact to pedal the remaining two days together as a unity tour between our two countries who had formerly been at war (even though only one of the countries actually knew about the conflict).

I was so buoyed by dinner that when one member of Team Germany casually mentioned that tomorrow's mileage was 106 miles, it almost didn't send me into sheer panic mode.

Almost.

Day 5
August 12, 2011

With 269 miles behind me, and 106 miles ahead of me, today was a day that I really had to dig down deep and access another gear. And that's not a metaphor. With the help of Annette, the woman on Team Germany, I actually found a gear on my bike I didn't know I had. This was not just any gear, but a gear that actually made the whole pedaling process infinitely easier. Annette named him Henry and it was love at first shift. Suddenly I was flying down the highway with great glee, passing other riders.

Now, you would think that with my newfound glee that I would feel a kinship with everyone else on the ride, an overwhelming desire to support my weary colleagues by yelling encouraging epithets. While I really did do that for most of the day, that first time I found and used Henry and started flying, it's possible that I didn't yell out a motivating cheer. It's possible that I heard myself yell out, "Later, bitches!" as I flew by Teams USA and Germany. I swear, for the rest of the day, I really did yell out distinctly more supportive cheers.

One thing I noticed today is that the topic of HIV/AIDS doesn't come up much on this ride. To compare California's AIDS/LifeCycle to this Charity Treks ride is like comparing apples and oranges. On the California event, there are twenty-five hundred riders who have to raise a minimum fundraising amount of thirty-five hundred dollars to participate. They sleep in a mobile city with the perimeter manned by security. All of the meals are professionally catered, and the meals are an all-you-can-eat gourmet experience. Nightly entertainment includes some celebrities who pop in and the screening of videotaped messages from celebrities who can't be there.

There are five hundred volunteer roadies on AIDS/LifeCycle cheering you on every step of the way. They perform every logistical function from the serving of the food to the picking-up of the trash to the setting up of the stages, all usually while wearing a different costume each and every day to keep the riders entertained and motivated. When the cyclists pedal through the Californian towns, the streets are often lined with citizens to cheer on and wave at the spectacle. Media coverage is everywhere.

HIV/AIDS is a real presence on AIDS/LifeCycle. There is a Dedication Tent in camp that exists as a quiet place of refuge to memorialize the fallen members of our community. There is a daily morning newsletter that details the needs of the beneficiaries. There is the presence of the Positive Peddlers, a group of riders proudly and visibly proclaiming their HIV status as they pedal to raise funds for services for those who can't afford much-needed care. The sense of urgency on AIDS/LifeCycle can be directly correlated to the need to raise funds and awareness to assist our brothers and sisters who so desperately need assistance.

Here are on Charity Treks, things are different. There are seventy riders with absolutely no fundraising minimum beyond the

$275.00 registration fee. We sleep in various public campsites and, for one night, we camp in one of our fellow participant's backyard. An incredible husband-and-wife team, Bruce and Elena, prepare the meals and strictly monitor your portions so there is enough food to go around. There are no celebrities to be found, neither in person nor via recorded message.

A crew of ten or so members set out some snacks and drive the vehicles in case someone needs a hand on the road. Sure, they cheer when you pull into a pit stop, but it's the clapping of a few hard-working folks not in costume. When we pedaled through the towns, we rarely merited a second glance from citizens, as we looked just like any other group of weekend cycling enthusiasts. There is no press coverage here on Charity Treks.

But, again, the big difference on Charity Treks is that you can almost get through the day without thinking about HIV/AIDS at all. To be clear, I love that this ride is specifically raising money to find a cure to HIV/AIDS. The funds go directly toward applying for seed grants that have the potential to turn into much larger research grants. This made for a far more persuasive fundraising appeal. I was able to raise thousands more dollars here on Charity Treks than I was able to for AIDS/LifeCycle, which raises money for services for HIV/AIDS-affected Californians who my East Coast friends and family would never meet. But seed grants are not a tangible presence you feel when you are out there pedaling on Charity Treks.

One of three organizers of this event is out about his HIV-positive status, and he says a few words at every third meal or so, but it sometimes reads far more tokenistic than it reads inspiring. The sense of urgency here on Charity Treks feels more correlated to the physical challenge of pedaling hundreds of miles than it is connected to HIV/AIDS.

Side by side, the apples and oranges comparison feels so much more like apples and orangutans. As I rode today, I thought more and more about ways to bring some of AIDS/LifeCycle into Charity Treks without tampering with the real culture of family and support that this small ride experience of Charity Treks evokes. I thought about changes that could increase their fundraising. I thought about changes that could raise awareness in the communities through which we were biking. I thought about anything and everything so that I didn't have to think about the fact that my legs were on all kinds of fire.

There were certainly some pretty insane hills today, but the hardest part for me physically was a downhill portion that featured a graded incline far more steep than anything I had previously experienced. Many of my fellow riders cited that mile down the steep hill as their favorite part of the day. They grinned as they flew through it. I grimaced as I gripped my brakes the entire time, truly scared I was going to go head over handlebars. It was the most memorable part of my day, but certainly not my favorite.

My favorite part was unquestionably the many miles Team USA and Team Germany covered together as a cohesive group. Without prompting, we rotated partners quite often, always finding someone new to talk to until it was time to rotate to someone else. It wasn't planned; it just organically went down like that. Somewhere in my head, I tried to process that I was biking both my second century in four days as well as my second century of my entire life. But the group dynamic allowed me to focus on these new bonds more than the road ahead. Plus, now I have Henry, the newfound bike gear, so nothing can go wrong.

We finished the ride by setting up our tents in an RV camp in rural Maine during their Luau weekend. That previous sentence is both 100 percent true as well as 100 percent surreal. We actually struck up conversation at dinner with a couple of the RV denizens and, by the end of the conversation, they had fished money out of their wallets to give to us to support our cause. It really was a beautiful thing. It almost made the overabundance of confederate flags seem unnoticeable.

At the very end of the day, I was told that tomorrow's ride is fifty-ish miles. I was feeling pretty good about that. That I wasn't freaked out was, on its own, nuts. A distance of fifty-ish miles is still longer than any of my training rides, but it feels distinctly doable given the hundreds and hundreds of miles I have already logged in over the past four days. And it feels even more doable because I have this amazing cocoon of support around me.

Tomorrow is the last day of Charity Treks and I'm anxious and fearful of finishing: anxious because my legs really are screaming at me, and fearful because I don't want to lose this group that has made things infinitely less blurry and indistinct. I'm told that the last day is usually pretty emotional for participants. I think I'm starting to see why. We will see where my head and heart end up.

Day 6
August 13, 2011

Last day. How is that even possible? My legs are screaming for me to end this madness but my heart is not quite ready for this experience to be over. I've conquered physical challenges, forged lasting relationships, and formed irrational and stalker-ish crushes.

Regarding that last bit, I should here admit that I have developed the most ridiculous crush on one of the men on Team Germany. He's a dreamy city planner who waxes on about bridges with the same fervency that I use to wax on about Wilson Phillips. That the other man on Team Germany is his fiancé really wasn't a part of my reality. I was able to subtract that minor fact from my narrative.

Also, the dreamy city planner bears a truly uncanny resemblance to my ex-husband, but I'm sure that's just a coincidence and didn't factor into my crush at all, right? Regardless, aside from the "He's taken" and "He's my ex-husband's twin" details, there was no way it was ever going to work out between us. The last thing I need is to tell my Jewish parents, "I fell in love with a man on Team Germany." It just wouldn't fly. Not now. Not ever.

Becoming so deeply infatuated and committed to a fleeting interaction with a distinctly unavailable gent is a special kind of sad, but it is still a pursuit into which I threw myself completely. It propelled me along. Right on the surface was the idea that maybe one day I'll find someone else. About a millimeter beneath the surface was the idea that maybe one day my ex-husband and I would be able to reconcile. Again, it all felt like a special kind of sad, but one I embraced nonetheless.

The last fifty-ish miles were actually a little difficult physically. I was chafed in unmentionable places. My left knee and I were in a really nasty fight in which harsh words were spoken that can never be taken back. My quads and I broke up on Day 3. But still, I kept on pedaling.

Honoring our internationally ratified treaty, Team USA and Team Germany rode together for the entirety of this last day. We were like a fierce gang—a nonthreatening gang that you and your elderly neighbors could totally take down. But, still, a gang. There was this melding of physical exertion and emotional investment that combined to form a complete experience. It would have been amazing to have pedaled together the whole ride starting on Day 1 back in Montréal, but I really am appreciative for the time we had together however shortened it had turned out to be.

After we finished 424 miles, a few police cars with flashing lights escorted all seventy riders the last mile to the Closing Ceremonies, located in a small park in the heart of Portland, Maine. It actually conveyed a nice sense of importance to the end of the ride. There was a smattering of folks lined up along the paths, clapping. I was pretty convinced that a good chunk of those folks didn't actually know what their claps supported, but claps without meaning sound pretty similar to supportive claps, so it worked. I rode in last, which felt right to me at the time.

It would be ideal to write all about how the Closing Ceremonies were cathartic, but I can't. I missed most of it. Right around the start of the proceedings, I looked around and it seemed that everyone on the ride was clasping a significant other. Now,

I knew for a fact that a ton of my fellow riders were single, but there they were at the Closing Ceremonies, clutching significant others. Everyone seemed to have someone except for me. The best explanation I could devise was that some sort of Portland-based social service agency was giving out significant others to the riders when they entered the park. As I was the last rider to enter the park, this Portland-based social service agency realized they had miscounted their stock of significant others and there weren't any partners left to distribute. A bummer for sure, but what could you do?

Then, two minutes after the proceedings commenced, the dreamy city planner and his partner grasped each other's hands. I simply could not look away. There was a part of me processing that there were doctors on stage highlighting all the great work being done to find a cure for HIV/AIDS, but I couldn't hear them. There was a part of me processing that there was a cyclist walking through the crowd high-fiving everyone to celebrate our accomplishments, but I couldn't see him. There was a part of me processing that I should feel amazing right now, but I couldn't feel it. The only thing in the world that I could process was the intertwined hands of these two men. And after I processed that image, I immediately lost it. Tears-running-down-my-cheek lost it.

Everything immediately went back to being blurry, back to being indistinct. It felt so overwhelming. I was angry that I was getting so upset but I couldn't get out of the way of my own emotional, oncoming train. I kept thinking, "I do not want to go back to my routine, to my life, to what lies imminently ahead." It was so overwhelming that I simply had to walk away. I stood fifty feet apart from the Closing Ceremonies, by myself, crying.

I was suddenly reminded why I sometimes end up detesting my participation in these rides: because they end. I keenly remember when I first did one of these multiday events ten years ago, there was an orientation video in which one of the participants proclaimed, "You will live for the next week like you want to live the other fifty-one weeks a year." I also remember scoffing at that line because, as a jaded gay Jew from New Jersey, that sentence was infinitely more aspirational than it was realistic. A few days later, at the end of that first event, I remember thinking, *Holy hell. It's true! This really is how I want to live the rest of my year!*

I really and genuinely liked who I was this week. I really and genuinely adored the people who surrounded me this week. I really and genuinely enjoyed every interaction I had this week. That's not my baseline at home. Here, I don't have to filter out noise to put things in perspective. At home, I can barely process a thought because the cacophony is so loud. On the other eight or nine events in which I have participated, I just accepted the end of the event. But here, standing fifty feet apart from the Closing Ceremonies crying by myself, I rebelled. For at least a few minutes.

My rebellion came in the form of a litany of questions. *What if I don't go back to Vermont, to the ruins, to the blurriness? What if I stay here in Portland with its amazing lunch spot that I ate at earlier this afternoon and its industry, about which I know nothing but which will doubtlessly support me, both financially and spiritually? What if I asked Team Germany and the rest of Team USA to stay with me? What if I never rode in a car for the rest of my life and only biked places thus always evoking this past week?* The stakes just felt so infinitely high in this situation, so I grasped at whatever I could to prolong the experience no matter how absurd the suggestion.

As I was grasping, the Closing Ceremonies ended and Team USA and Team Germany walked over to me together. I had obviously separated myself from the group and looked pretty emotional. They sensed it, crossed the fifty-foot divide, and were so comforting and supportive. When the group hug happened, my rebelling and grasping ceased and I let out a deep and audible sigh. The ride was over. My promise had been fulfilled.

In that moment, and these many hours later, I'm convinced that the answers I needed could be found in that exhalation of breath: the answer to rebuilding the mess, fixing my flat tires, re-attaching my chains, climbing the hills, achieving inter-country collaboration, finding my Henry Gear, and perpetuating that which I don't want to end. The sigh was an acknowledgment that change was possible. The sigh was an admission that even though I do some stupid things when I dive headfirst into very shallow waters, some good can actually come out of that reckless approach. The sigh was a commemoration of the sense of community, feelings of accomplishment, and an actual fulfillment of my foolhardy promise.

The rest of the day went by way too quickly. The hot shower was bliss both because it was a hot shower and because it was located in the hotel room that Teams USA and Germany decided to share. There was a dinner and an auction. And there was dancing at a gay club. The six of us headed back to the hotel together and gabbed the night away until, one by one, we fell asleep. I'm sitting on the bathroom floor penning these last few words because I know that the experience will definitely end when the first member of our group needs to depart for the train station in only three hours.

I keep coming back to that sigh and the reality that comes along with it: I can't avoid returning to Vermont. I can't escape the circumstances that led to my being on this bike ride. I can't hide from the emotional reckoning on the immediate horizon that I need to confront. I can't stay here in Portland. I can't stay with these amazing people.

The only thing I can do is to keep on pedaling. The only thing I have to do is to keep on pedaling. The only thing that will get me through all of this is to keep on pedaling. And if I keep on pedaling, maybe, just maybe, I will get there. I don't exactly know where "there" is right now. I'm pretty sure it's at the top of the next hill. If I keep on pedaling, I am confident that I really will find out what's waiting for me at the summit.

Of Sea Lions and Hippie Retreats

(Monterey and Big Sur, California:
October 23, 2011 – October 29, 2011)

Day 1
October 23, 2011

I am broken.

There are countless other ways to express it, but that's the expression that feels right. I realize how hopeless and pathetic it sounds, so I really did try out some other phrases. But none of them matched up with what was going on with me.

"I am off track" makes me feel like a corrective course could easily be located if I just put in the effort to locate it.

"I am lost" suggests that an inner compass could easily be found if I just put in the effort to find it.

"I am stuck" just wants for some easily applied emotional lubricant if I just put in the effort to . . . um . . . lubricate it.

So instead, I am broken. I know that the idiom is extreme, but I actually am taking small comfort in the fact that I haven't inserted the word "irrevocably" at the head of the phrase, which would turn an extreme set of three words into a hopeless gang of four.

I'm trying to believe that the reason for my state of brokenness is less important than the fact of my state of brokenness, especially as the reason is so unbelievably uncomplicated. The past five months can be boiled down to this simple narrative: I had a relationship. I built my life on that relationship. I lost that relationship. And somewhere after and as a result of that loss, I broke.

Not that you would necessarily know that I am broken to watch me bustle about this small town in Vermont. I'm told that my curse is the gift for which some of my broken brethren strive: I can compartmentalize like no one else and keep right on functioning. I can decry an inaccurate newspaper headline about me. I can talk a student off a ledge. I can interview a hero on my gay radio show. I can just generally plow forward at a rushed pace, without stopping. Because to stop would be to pause. To pause would be to think. To think would be to realize that I'm alone.

And to realize that I'm alone would be to let the waves of being broken wash all over me.

If you stopped watching me and tried talking to me, now that would quickly lead you to the conclusion that something is rotten in the state of Schneckmark. I really haven't had much control over my mouth these past few months. To be clear, my baseline filter doesn't normally do a ton of filtering. But, if you have even casually locked eyes with me in the past five months, you would have borne witness to the fact that said filter has been doing even less filtering than it normally filters. And by "borne witness," I mean something more like, "been held hostage."

I have actually seen the fear in people's eyes when the words tumble out of my mouth with no end in sight. I would be screaming in my head: *Shut up! For the love of all things holy. Shut. Up!* But even as I hear the screaming in my head, I can also hear my own voice rambling on incessantly. I think I should maybe carry pre-stamped postcards around with me so that my verbal captives can at least send a missive to their friends and family to let them know that they miss them and hope to see them soon.

After a few months of bustling about and rambling at anyone who had not yet learned to avoid me, I ended up on the covered porch of an earth-goddess-acquaintance of mine. She's the kind of woman I don't know super well but still exudes the serenity I want to emulate but doubt I could ever convincingly evoke. She's the kind of woman who puts her hand on my arm and tells me that I am being me and being me is always the best process of being that I could ever be. She's the kind of woman who, after she speaks, I just want to say, "Namaste" even though I don't really say things like "Namaste" and actually roll my eyes each time when we say it at the end of a Bikram class—which, you'll recall, was a prior goal of mine, and a practice to which I am now addicted.

On that covered porch, with the rain beating down, I again word-vomited my brokenness. She gently offered the idea of attending a healing workshop at the Esalen Institute in Big Sur, California. Without doing much research, I, of course, booked this trip. Sure, Esalen's website looked like a haven for hippies. Sure, healing workshops are not typically the way I approach moving through life. Sure, Esalen really did look like a haven for hippies. But my earth-goddess-acquaintance told me it would be healing. It was direction. It was concrete. It was thus all the convincing I needed. Namaste.

So here I sit, perched on a stone ledge overlooking the bay in Monterey, California. I am far, far away from the East Coast. I really need to be geographically far, far away from the East Coast. Vermont had become completely haunted; there was a new and unexpected trigger around each and every corner, usually in the form of my ex-husband's blue Yaris. Yes, there are a lot of Blue Yarises (Yarii?) out there, but this is Brattleboro, Vermont, population: 2. Odds are, when that blue Yaris whizzes by, it's him behind the wheel. And even when there wasn't a vehicular sighting, I was still on the lookout. I couldn't go to the award-winning Brattleboro Farmers' Market without first taking a tour of the parking lot to take an auto inventory. Yes, there are a lot of people in this world, but this is Brattleboro, Vermont, population: 2. Odds are, if the award-winning Brattleboro Farmers' Market is in session, he's there. I had to escape Vermont and I had to escape Vermont quickly.

Booking this trip didn't feel like it would be enough, so I opted to cash in a few weeks of my months of unused vacation time to flee the Green Mountain/Blue Yaris State. I spent a few days in Baltimore with Team Germany and a few more with my parents in New Jersey before arriving today at this keystone of my time away: a healing retreat in California. Tomorrow, a van will pick me up to deliver me to the promise of healing, an activity I most definitely need given my current state.

This feels like a different type of writing than my time in Uganda or on the 425-mile bike ride. For those processes of chronicling, I felt like a thing apart, an alien with a snarky observation about the activity that was going on all around me. Sure, there was certainly some self-reflection, but I tried my darnedest to focus both on my surroundings as well as what I saw that was broken therein. But now, that which is broken is *me* and it's going to be difficult to misdirect a reader's attention to a Ugandan nurse or a flat bike tire.

Which is not to say that I won't still try to distract you! For example, there is a sea lion on a rock right in front of me. Right this very second. A sea lion staring into my eyes, boring into my soul. I am utterly convinced that somewhere in this silent exchange between the broken gay Jew and the sea lion is the key to it all. I'm suddenly and desperately clinging to a metaphor that is as fabricated and ridiculous as it is wanted and needed. It's all about the sea lion. I'm convinced of it. But, ultimately, what do I know? I'm the guy who needs healing and will take it anywhere I can get it.

So, heed me, Sea Lion! I'm going to go to this hippie retreat and keep the image of you fresh in my mind and maybe, just maybe, this is all going to work. Do you hear me, Sea Lion? Are you reading these words, suddenly literate Sea Lion? Change is coming. And there will be a reckoning between you and I. When you next see me, I will be whole again. Until we meet again, Sea Lion.

Day 2
October 24, 2011

"**H**e makes jokes, but he's in a fuckload of pain."
Those words were actually said today. About me. Now there was certainly a lot that happened since I woke up this morning. Truly, it was a jam-packed day where a veritable ton went down. But all I can think about is that one sentence, directed at me, which completely and utterly disarmed me and laid me low. I'll try to recap the events that led up to that eleven-word annihilation, but it will always be hanging pall-like over this entry. As it was a sentence that was launched at the end of the day, I will endeavor to start at the beginning. But know that though I make jokes, I am in a fuckload of pain.

So much of this day was me just feeling and acting like a wide-eyed, nervous child about to head to his first day of hippie school. A fellow Gear & Tent Roadie from AIDS/LifeCycle came down from San Francisco to hang out for a few hours by the bay in full view of my sea lion nemeses. He knew I was nervous about Esalen and he tried to calm me down. We both acknowledged that calming me down was a futile effort. After he left, I walked from my hotel to the van stop with my suitcase in tow, questioning every few steps of the three-block walk. When I arrived at the designated pickup location, I checked the printout of the confirmation email three times, scanned the street signs three times to confirm my location, and checked a map three times to confirm that the street signs were the correct confirmation of the confirmation email.

The van to Esalen arrived and all hopes of the smells of incense and the sounds of chanting were dashed against the reality of it being just a normal ten-passenger van. It was the kind of van that gets you and another small group to and from a destination, not the kind of van that heals your broken heart. There was nary a tie-dyed motif in sight.

I was excited to lay my eyes on the other passengers to see what these folks would be like. *Would these be my people?* kept running through my head. If the demography of the van was any indication, I deduced that I would most certainly be in a gender minority: I was the only male of the nine passengers.

The ride along the cliffs from Monterey to Big Sur was visually stunning. Unfortunately, the scenery and Zen potential was tarnished by one of the other passengers talking incessantly, seemingly without direction or substance, but constant nonetheless. I wanted to just relax, but the chattering would not stop. Even more unfortunately, the passenger who wouldn't shut the hell up was me.

I was not without awareness of my runaway train-of-a-mouth, but the chasm between my thoughts and my mouth was Mariana Trench-like. As words were flying out of my mouth, all I kept

thinking was, *Ken, stop talking! Seriously! Stop. Talking. Hey, look!
You're talking again. And then there you go again with more of the
talking! Please stop talking?* Ultimately, my nervous energy main-
tained that disconnect between tempered thoughts and uncontrol-
lable motormouth.

When our van slowed down as we approached Esalen, I too
slowed down. And when we stopped, mercifully for all my fellow
passengers, I stopped yammering. I checked in at the front desk
and confirmed that I was indeed registered for two separate workshops: a five-day healing journey and a two-and-a-half day meditation adventure. I followed the path to my bunk and dumped
my stuff in my room. The room was four sets of bunk beds but it
didn't look like anyone else's items were present, so I was excited
to have a big space to myself.

Somehow the day had flown by and it was already dinner-
time, so I proceeded directly to the main lodge. The meal was
incredible: extraordinarily hearty, locally grown, and vegetarian
friendly. I filled up my tray with great enthusiasm, as dinner was
quite the culinary delight. That positive energy quickly dissipated
when I turned around to find a place to sit. Suddenly, it was like I
was back in the high school cafeteria all over again. And oh, how
I hated the Pascack Hills High School cafeteria.

The Esalen cafeteria had cliques both strange and familiar. To
the right were the spiritual kids who I think were chanting Ohm
between bites. Straight in front of me were the cool kids, all of whom
were on my earlier van ride and none of whom were making eye
contact with Captain Ken Chatterbox. To the left were a group of
smiley, young folks. They were laughing and grinning and seemed
like a pretty inclusive hive, so I beelined it for their table. They were
so unbelievably welcoming, inviting me into their laughing, smiling,
inclusive klatch. I was feeling great. Well, at least, I was feeling great
until the woman next to me asked me to describe the job I had been
hired to do at Esalen. Then I wasn't feeling so great anymore.

Turns out, with dozens and dozens of tables to choose from,
I had managed to sit down at the table of volunteers who were

starting a month-long, work-learning program. This dinner was their orientation and welcome. When I explained that I was here to attend a workshop, the laughing ceased, the smiles faded, and the inclusivity disappeared. I was politely asked to leave the table as—and this is an actual quote—"Volunteers and workshop attendees are on different paths." I was a Shark. They were the Jets. Tonight, tonight, there'd be no dining together tonight. So I skulked away, tray in hand, head bowed.

I immediately saw an empty spot across from an ethereal, waif-like woman draped in Grecian robes. I sat right down at her table and I was prepared to be dazzled by her chi and her chakras. I instantly deduced that this was my Oracle of Big Sur Delphi and I was ready and open to receive her wisdom. Sadly, I think maybe the Oracle was out on break because this woman did not look up from her food. Not once. I smiled. I cleared my throat. I said hello. But there was no wisdom to be dispensed. So, much like lunch at Pascack Hills High School, I fled the cafeteria as quickly as I could.

As I had some time to kill before my workshop started tonight, I decided to check out the mineral baths for which Esalen is widely known. I remember reading on the website that the hot springs had healing powers. I also recall reading the phrase, "clothing optional." Well, the water might very well have had healing powers, but I didn't have the courage to find out. Turns out, the "clothing optional" description was a bit misleading. A more accurate description would have been, "FYI: not one person will be wearing clothes. At any point. If you're gay, you might see body parts of the opposite sex that you have only encountered in popular media or used as metaphors in a well-crafted essay. Given that, please be advised: this might be a jarring experience to see a parade of these parts on display. Your comfort with this is optional." So, much like the locker room at Pascack Hills High School, I fled as quickly as I possibly could. An hour later, it was time to start my five-day workshop.

Alright.

Deep breath.

Here we go.

The workshop was entitled, "The Courage to Be You: Letting Go and Moving On." It was subtitled—and I wish I were kidding here—"It's Time: No One Is Coming to Save You." The main title felt support-based. The subtitle was distinctly more fear- and shame-based.

Our facilitator for the week is named Mary. She is a licensed clinical psychologist, maybe five-foot-one in heels, seventy-five-years-old-ish, and a total spitfire. From the minute she started speaking, it was clear that she was a spitfire who does not tolerate bullshit. This, of course, makes me nervous. Also, she kept insinuating that she once provided a counseling session to Kanye West when they were on a hike in Sonoma. So there was that.

As she was introducing the work we would be doing together for the upcoming week, my eyes drifted around the room to the circle of seated participants. My initial demographic evaluation in the van wasn't too far off. This twenty-person workshop was only 10 percent male: one other guy and me. The age range of the participants seemed to be all over the map. And there was a woman a few seats away from me who already had tears running down her cheeks. So that made me nervous.

I refocused more fully when I heard Mary say, "So what I want you to do is . . . ." The activity was a simple one: stand, find someone else in the room with whom you wanted to spend time, grab his or her hand, and sit down. And, get this all done without speaking.

I froze. It felt like immediate chaos as people launched into the activity. I'm not a launcher when it comes to locking eyes and grabbing hands. I am usually infinitely more comfortable observing chaos and writing snarky things about it in my journal a few hours later. In the few seconds during which I was frozen—eight or nine seconds tops—there were nine pairs of people holding hands and sitting down. The only people left standing with no hands in our hands were me and one other woman. I immediately decided that she was my workshop soulmate. We had both hesitated. We both were observers. We both needed each other. We were destined to be together for at least the next five days and likely for the rest of our days on this planet.

Sadly, she had read our shared horoscope differently. She looked at me. She looked around the room to confirm there was no one else left standing. She looked back at me. And then she shrugged.

Seriously, she shrugged.

It was an unequivocal body movement roughly the same as her pulling out a megaphone and announcing, "Okay. Fine. Whatever." Although there was a huge chunk of me that was mortified by her reaction, most of me found her response to be slightly amusing. I have respect for all things direct. I reached out my hand, she grabbed the tips of my fingers, and we sat down. I was feeling pretty confident that she was not going to be my workshop soulmate. I was feeling exponentially more confident that she felt the same way.

After we were all seated, Mary asked us to volunteer to answer questions about our process during the activity: why did we select the person we selected? What was it like to grab another person's hand? How did it feel to sit down together? As each person individually described his or her experience, Mary would follow up by cutting right through to how the process mirrored the person's approach to life. We were barely forty minutes into this workshop and Mary had participants in tears because her analysis stripped them down to their core. Their method of interacting with other humans was laid bare on the table for the other nineteen strangers to witness. I had already started thinking about my process, what that might say about me, and how I wasn't quite ready to share. So I did the mature thing: I tried to wait out Mary. I refrained from volunteering and tried to run out the clock on tonight's session. It was already getting pretty late, so I thought this would be a winning strategy.

But this was not Mary's first rodeo. Kanye probably didn't get away with that strategy during their hike in Sonoma and neither would I. When we were about halfway though the group volunteering to share, Mary the Mind Reader announced, "By the way, we will stay here until everyone shares."

I went third to last and my turn was long. The length was not my own doing. It felt like Mary was pushing me hard, a fact confirmed at one point when Mary said, "I know I'm pushing you hard." She got me to share some details of my brokenness that the closest confidantes in my life didn't know. I couldn't get it out of my head that this sharing was happening in front of twenty strangers: Mary, my shrugging ex-soulmate, and eighteen others I didn't yet know. Thus, at one point, when I was feeling particularly backed into a corner, I did what I do: I made a joke. I can't remember exactly what I said, but I remember it being a stock line on which I could always count to get a laugh. And it did get a laugh. Mary laughed too. And then she said it.

"He makes jokes, but he's in a fuckload of pain."

The laughter died immediately. And Mary moved on to the next participant.

After the last person had shared, it was after 11:00 p.m. and I was completely spent. I hesitated to get up, not because I didn't want to leave but because I was really a bit out of it. Mary walked straight over to me and crouched down so that we were on eye level. "I know you," she said. "I know this pain. I've worked with this pain." She just seemed so confident about what this week could be for me if I was open to it. Then, just like that, she said good night and left me alone in the room.

In that moment, sitting on the floor, alone in a room in Big Sur, California, I resolved to try to be open. In that moment, I tried to put aside my doubts. In that moment, I chose to trust that Esalen could do wonders for me. In that moment, I believed I could heal.

93

Day 3
October 25, 2011

For the record, I really am trying. I am trying to be present. I am trying to go deep. I am trying to dance when the music is played.

And lest you think that the dancing and music were metaphors, oh how wrong you would be. When we entered the room this morning after breakfast (I sat with some folks from my session! It was nice! Take that, Pascack Hills!), Mary began by speaking passionately on the importance of dancing. She explained that it is crucial that we give our inner child a chance to play at the start of each day so that our inner adult can focus more fully on the work for the hours ahead. Then, before we had a chance to question whether this was a vague parable to decipher, Mary whipped out an old-school, circa 1998 CD player. She pressed play and, being gay, I immediately recognized the opening notes of Irene Cara's 1984 Oscar-winning anthem "Flashdance . . . What a Feeling." Even more hilarious, it was a cheap, knock-off remix of Irene Cara's 1984 Oscar-winning anthem. That wasn't Irene Cara singing and this version definitely did not win an Oscar. It was suddenly like the gayest and most low-rent Bar Mitzvah ever.

Mary didn't come right out and command us to dance. But when she started dancing herself, most everyone followed suit. How could you not? That is, unless you were me. I didn't fully throw myself into it; the surreal element of the scene was simply far too much for me to not be wide-eyed and frozen. But I did move my hips a bit and maybe clapped a few times. For me, in that room with that song playing, my slight movements were a full-on, Ken Schneck-on-Solid-Gold choreographed routine.

After the song faded out, Mary closed the dancehall and told us it was time to get to work. The crux of the day was spent identifying and addressing our Defenses: those coping methods that we have always put into place that we think are helping, but are actually causing us problems. About thirty Defenses were listed, and we had to identify our top three through a combination of assessment, dialogue, and what we know in our hearts to be true. Most everyone had the same experience of reading the list of Defenses and saying, "Oh. Yeah. Those would be mine." I was no exception.

My three Defenses were oh-so-clearly The Entertainer, The Perfectionist, and The Intellectualizer. I didn't need to read their descriptions to know they were my very best friends; their titles alone were convincing enough. Then, I read their descriptions and confirmed that they were indeed my very best friends. I could feel them seated beside me in that room.

The next step of the process was to talk to our Defenses and try to convince them to take an extended holiday from our lives, a permanent one if possible. Mary explained that, sure, we could just think through the activity in our heads. But if we really wanted to make progress on addressing our issues more authentically, we should have an actual, out-loud conversation with our three Defenses. And not just an actual, out-loud conversation, but a dialogue in which we anticipated how our Defenses would respond and counter with what we thought would be effective responses.

Immediately, The Entertainer, The Perfectionist, and The Intellectualizer got together and crafted a witty, meticulously composed, and über-cerebral memo outlining their collective doubt that I could live without them. It was a bulleted list that pretty much amounted to them scoffing at me for even approaching a process where the end result would be my leaving them behind. One of those bullets somehow worked in a priest, a rabbi, and a duck walking into a mineral bath, all of it underscored with a corresponding adult development theory. And each bullet was time stamped.

Look, I know my Defenses, and I know how they would respond. Heck, I even really did compose that fake, preemptive strike of a memo that I was pretty sure my Defenses would write. But when I sat in the corner and spoke with them individually, it was actually an engaging and nigh-revelatory exercise.

The Entertainer needed to be convinced that people could like him even if he lets his sad and broken side shine through. The Perfectionist needed to be shown that the earth would actually not stop rotating on its axis, even if I were being honest about both how much I had messed up in my past alongside the reality that I couldn't actually change it. And The Intellectualizer just needed to be told to shut the fuck up. My three foes weren't permanently banished to the hinterlands in the short time I sat with them, but it made me feel a might bit more confident that they could be controlled. For that, I was appreciative.

My sessionmates and I had lunch a bit later and when we returned, Mary greeted us solemnly and asked us to sit down. She said she had some "serious news for us." I couldn't imagine what it could be. Was it a national crisis? Was there a shortage of tempeh in the cafeteria? Was my ex-husband behind the curtain ready to jump out and welcome me back with open arms?

No, it was none of those. Mary looked at us gravely and said, "I'm sorry, but Ingrid has left us." Some people in the group gasped. Others said, "Aww!" Others just looked sad. I wasn't quite sure what to feel because I had no idea who Ingrid was. In fact, I wasn't sure if Ingrid was a real person, or if, "I'm sorry, but Ingrid has left us" was some sort of hippie code for something else. It was all very, "The red dog flies at night," evoking a covert Cold War secret mission.

I turned to the woman next to me and whispered, "Who was Ingrid?"

She laughed and replied, "The woman you held hands with last night."

Oh. Her.

Ingrid had left our healing workshop to join a yoga workshop. Farewell, Ingrid. My one-time soulmate. I will most certainly miss what we had: the way you shrugged your shoulders at me, the look in your eyes that I couldn't see because you never made eye contact, the way you so barely touched my hand. Namaste, Ingrid.

After we recovered from this earth-shattering news, Mary informed us that there was only one activity on the docket for the rest of the day. But it was, of course, a super intense one. We had to find a partner and reveal various truths about our lives to this person who was only slightly-less-than-a-stranger. When one person finished sharing, the other person would respond with an earnest, "Thank you." We rotated around the room many times, sharing four or five truths about our lives to seven or so partners. By chance, I ended up with partners who were willing to immediately reveal some truly deep-rooted issues and anguish. Or, everyone in the room was like that and there was no luck of the draw involved. Either way, I then had to share deep-rooted issues and anguish of my own. How could I not? I would have looked like an ass if the conversation had resembled anything like this:

PARTNER 1: I'm a three-time cancer survivor.
KEN: Thank you. I really like tennis.
PARTNER 1: Thank you.

<rotate>

PARTNER 2: I came home one day to find my husband hanging from a tree in the backyard.
KEN: Thank you. I sleep with a stuffed cow named Cow and a stuffed elephant named Elephant.
PARTNER 2: Thank you.

<rotate>

PARTNER 3: I barely made it out of a fire and will always have burn scars covering a huge chunk of my body.
KEN: Thank you. I can throw an incredible Chinese-food-themed dinner party without anyone ever knowing it was a 100 percent vegan meal.
PARTNER 3: Thank you.

I should also note that I immediately felt out of place in this group as those were very real truths above that were shared with me by my various partners. Cancer, suicide, fire, and so much more. And I'm here . . . why? Because my marriage ended? I feel like an overdramatic charlatan. Now, I did reveal quite a bit more than I ever thought I ever would, including the very real and inexcusable role I played in the demise of my relationship. But, still, I felt like a drama queen whose issues paled in comparison to the deep pain in the room.

The other piece of this exercise took place whenever we acquired a new partner. Before any truths or acknowledgments were exchanged, we had to look into each other's eyes for a full minute. Turns out, sixty seconds can feel astronomically longer than I ever would have thought possible. For Partner 1, I almost immediately looked away. I met Partner 2's eyes for seven or so seconds. Partner 3 got a good chunk of the minute with my eyes gazing into hers, but I was laughing on the inside and grinning like an idiot on the outside.

But then Partner 4 came along with an undeniable earnestness. It was palpable. Without saying a word, her energy encouraged me to really try to pull off full-on eye contact. So I gave in, let go, and looked into her eyes for the full sixty seconds. It was incredible: I felt like we had forged a very real connection that deepened the truths I shared and enhanced the gratitude of my thank-yous.

We all went to dinner as a group and left dinner as a group. Standing outside of the main lodge, I turned down multiple offers to go to the baths. It was enough that I got naked with my truths; I was pretty far from ready to get naked with my body.

After dinner, I did, however, go for an incredible run along the highway above the staggeringly beautiful cliffs of Big Sur. I ran farther than I had originally planned. I wanted to keep my body in motion because to stop would be to consider what I shared today and to confront the truths I had always known but had never before voiced. I felt like I was at capacity for the day, so I just kept on running.

My physical exhaustion coupled with my mental fatigue now have me ready to go to sleep and, amazingly, have The Intellectualizer, The Perfectionist, and the Entertainer all plum tuckered out. For now, they're keeping their mouths shut and the silence is golden.

Day 4

October 26, 2011

At breakfast this morning, I voiced my relief to my dining mates about how great it was to enter the dining lodge with the knowledge that I would have individuals with whom I could unquestionably share a table. The eight-part harmony that was organically created when everyone else immediately responded "Me too!" rivaled any professional choir you could possibly find. It was as comical as it was validating. I entered this morning's workshop on a high and even danced for a few seconds when not-Irene-Cara sang us into our morning. Sadly, that high did not last very long.

The first activity Mary laid out in front of us was pretty simple. We had to partner up and get back into our eye-gazing routine. As I was now an old pro at looking into souls via their irises, I felt ready for whatever instruction was about to come next. It was a simple set of directions: the taller member of the pair was to ask "Please?" and the shorter member was to respond "No," all the while as both of them held each other's gaze. There were to be no embellishments on the script. Just a "Please?" and a response of "No."

As I was the tallest of the now nineteen (I miss you, Ingrid!) of us in the workshop, it always fell to me to ask "Please?" and consequently it was also always me who was met with the answer of "No." Suddenly two of my Defenses woke up and I chuckled at the simplicity of the activity even as I tried to decipher the significance of what this activity could do to heal me. For the first three exchanges, I was completely detached. I thought it was silly, as the script was so irrevocably etched in stone.

Then, between the third and fourth exchange, my buddy The Perfectionist joined the game. Suddenly I was in it to win it and, for me, winning meant trying to somehow get my partner to say something other than "No." Ideally, I wanted to hear a "Yes," but an "Okay, I'll consider it" would do just fine.

I threw myself into the activity and tried various intonations and facial expressions in order to get my activity partner to change her response even just one time. But she stood resolute, looked into my eyes, and said "No." I then tried changing the question mark into a period, morphing my "Please" into a statement. But my partner stood resolute, looked into my eyes, and said "No." I then tried changing the period into an exclamation point, morphing my "Please" into a demand. But my partner stood resolute, looked into my eyes and said "No."

Then, somewhere in there, the activity stopped being a game and started cutting me up emotionally. So much of my state of being broken was about wanting something I didn't and couldn't have, no matter how hard I tried to get it back. It felt both frustrating and miserable to now be in another situation where my efforts were being soundly rebuffed. Why can't I make myself clear to this woman in front of me? Why can't she just give me what I want? Doesn't she see how much this is tearing me apart? To her credit, she did instantly pick up on how frantic and panicky I had suddenly become. Even though her response never wavered, each "No" became drenched in progressively more compassion.

When Mary finally stopped the activity, my forehead sported a sheen of sweat; I really had thrown myself into the task and actually felt somewhat breathless and wholly defeated. Needless to say, I was happy for Mary's cessation, as I was hoping that we were moving on to something different with which I could have both more control as well as a little more distance from my anxiety.

But Mary wasn't done with this activity quite yet.

Mary instructed the nineteen of us to change things up by simply adding one more word to the script: the taller person had to add the word "Stay" after the word "Please." Immediately, the reality of what was about to happen slammed right into me. Although my ego certainly knew that this exercise was for the entire group, it sliced me right to the core. I knew with great certainty that, within moments, I was going to be a mess.

There had to have been less than a minute between Mary's new rule and our resumption of the task at hand, but it felt like an eternity. I felt crushed and we hadn't even started yet. From the very first "Please stay" I threw out at my partner, I was desperate. I wasn't so far gone in delusion that I didn't know what answer was coming my way, but it didn't matter. My "Please stay"s were full of mourning. My "Please stay"s were wracked with guilt. My "Please stay"s were bordering on lunacy. I didn't really know this woman who served as my partner in this exercise, but she wasn't the person I saw across from me.

And she knew it.

She knew exactly what was going on—the whole group knew about my divorce—each "No" she offered up in response was more gentle than the last. I was clawing at the brick wall in front of me, and she was doing her part to pad the wall while always maintaining its impenetrability. This exercise went on for countless minutes and it wasn't long before her eyes welled up in tears. I thought her emotional response was going to be my opening, but my manipulation didn't work here. She just kept answering "No" and I couldn't understand why. It didn't matter anymore that these were the rules; I barely even remembered that she was only doing exactly what she was instructed to do. I couldn't make my case. I couldn't sway her. And I was devastated.

Other stuff happened today. I mean, an absolute ton of other stuff happened today, as everything I just described was only the opening activity. But nothing else mattered. Nothing else registered. Nothing else was as important as the three-word exchange that destroyed me ten hours ago.

Please stay?

No.

Day 5
October 27, 2011

So I walked out today. I'm not proud of it. Really, I'm not. But I did it anyway and I did it without any hesitation.

This morning's activity was a laying-on of hands: a literal laying-on of hands that trumped any metaphors that could possibly be evoked. Actual hands. Of other people. On me.

Holy hell: no.

I would like to pause here and say that I really didn't know these other workshop participants very well. First, we have only known each other for three days. Granted, it has been an intense three days and, yes, I have fallen in and out of love in less than seventy-two hours before in my life. But I really didn't feel like I knew these people very well. Also, I still overwhelmingly felt like I was a fraud in this group. The more I heard about everyone else's real and deep traumas, the louder I screamed in my head, *Suck it up, Ken! It's just a breakup!* It was not a coincidence that the two women with whom I bonded most closely were the ones who I perceived to have the lowest level of trauma in the group. This is not to say that I didn't enjoy their company immensely (I did), but it didn't hurt that I felt distinctly less like a con artist with them.

Thus, when Mary divvied us into groups of three and I wasn't with either of those two women, I was slightly bummed. When Mary then informed us that the upcoming activity would involve hands all over us, I was more than slightly panicked. I was already starting to lose my focus and I didn't even know what we would be doing.

Mary laid out one pallet in front of each group. Well, at least, she called them "pallets." In reality, they were those stiff and unyielding tri-fold exercise mats we had in gym class that Velcroed together so that the schoolboys could practice wrestling while the schoolgirls (and Ken Schneck) did somersaults. Seeing that mat laid out in front of me really brought me back to my gym class discomfort, which is never really a solid frame of mind to hold when entering into an activity that may lead to healing.

Mary asked for volunteers to lay on the pallet first. Other than the knowledge that there would be hands on us, we didn't know anything else about what was going to go down on the pallet. My group of three hesitated. One member of my group, with pupils more dilated than mine, shook her head no. The other, after a pause in which she noted my hesitation, said, "I don't mind going first." But this kind soul had already been exposed over the past three days as a tireless giver who gives until she has nothing left to offer. I think her three Defenses were The Martyr, The Savior, and The Defender. In that moment, it didn't feel right to make her give more, so I heard myself say, "No, I'll do it." It was about 97 percent not wanting her to give more and 3 percent actually of me wanting to lie on that pallet. And I'm being generous with that 3 percent. But lie on that pallet I did.

Mary's first instruction for the two people not laying on the pallet was to have them kneel next to the sprawled-out volunteers. My two activity partners kneeled shoulder to shoulder on my left side and looked awkwardly down at me. Before I had a chance to look away—as I am wont to do when there are two people looking awkwardly down at me—those of us lying down were instructed to make eye contact with those kneeling next to us. Mary instructed us to fix in our mind's eye who we needed them to be in that moment.

Honestly, I had no clue who I really needed them to be, but my first fleeting thought was that the two women kneeling next to me were my parents. And then, once I thought they were my parents, a narrative immediately took root that I just couldn't shake. These weren't just my parents, but they were my parents at my Bar Mitzvah. Then it wasn't just my Bar Mitzvah, but some point during my Bar Mitzvah when I accidentally fell to the floor and kept on reciting the prayers. And there were my parents, kneeling by my side, so sad that I had fallen down but so proud that my status on the ground did not prevent me from executing all the

Judaism to which I had been spiritually bound to carry out. The whole experience of having those two women kneeling next to me felt so weird, but somehow the even weirder plot I had concocted helped me adapt to all the weirdness.

After what seemed like an eternity of staring up at my "parents," Mary instructed the volunteers to turn over on their stomachs. I was relieved to break eye contact and relaxed my body as I flipped over on that pallet. That relaxation only lasted a fraction of a second, as Mary instructed the kneeling pairs to give the volunteer's back a good rub. My body went instantly rigid as I threw myself into panic mode.

I am not quite sure I can articulate exactly what so supremely threw me off there, but I think it was a combination of strangers' hands on me, not really knowing the people whose hands were on me, and the fact that there were individuals I really didn't know whose hands were rubbing me. Don't be fooled: I am a total and complete sucker for a great massage, but this context felt wrong and once I convinced myself it was wrong, the rubbing was intolerable from that first touch through every endless minute.

To be clear, there was nothing seedy or untoward about the activity and it wasn't markedly different than one of those standing massage circles you might find at a professional development activity. But I had just pictured these two women as my parents and now they were rubbing me. And even if they weren't my parents, they were two women. And even if I was okay with them being women, they were still two women I didn't know. It just didn't work. On any level.

Mary's last instruction was for us volunteers to return to lying on our backs. She asked us to imagine the presence in that room of the individual with whom we most needed to have a conversation. When that person was in our mind, we were told to just start talking to them out loud. It wasn't clear if we were supposed to look at the two participants kneeling next to us, but you couldn't help but feel their presence, particularly as they were kneeling right there next to you. So I did what any infant who feels overwhelmed would do: I closed my eyes and tried to shut it all out.

Let's recap the scene here. I'm lying on a gym mat with my eyes closed. Two strangers are kneeling next to me and gripping one of my shoulders in support. I knew I needed to have a conversation with my ex-husband. At this point, the women next to me knew I needed to have a conversation with my ex-husband. Heck, anybody with whom I have crossed paths in the past few months knew I needed to have a conversation with my ex-husband. I fixed the image of him in my mind and tried over and over again to work the activity but the words wouldn't come out. I could hear the volunteers in other groups having their conversations out loud, but I just laid there in silence. My mouth tried to form words, but the words wouldn't come out. My "parents" kneeling next to me gripped my shoulder even more tightly in support, but the words wouldn't come out. I thought maybe the activity would help the healing process, but the words wouldn't come out.

These were obviously crucial conversations in our lives, so Mary set aside forty-five minutes for us to have our conversations. Forty. Five. Minutes. For those poor women kneeling next to me, that meant forty-five minutes of me lying there with my eyes closed uttering nary a peep. I felt terrible for them, as it had to have been insanely awkward, but, again, I just couldn't make the words come out. When Mary rang the bell signifying the end of this phase of the activity, I opened my eyes and looked at my two partners. I instantly apologized. They hugged me right there on the ground.

When I stood up, I felt immediately dizzy and, with zero hesitation whatsoever, I left the room. This wasn't break time. I simply just got up and walked out. I found a patch of grass many pathways away from our meeting space and crumpled to the ground. Sixteen percent of my leaving was my being horribly lost in that imaginary conversation; my brain was whirling from the fact that I, a jabbermouth wordsmith, couldn't make any sounds come out. But 84 percent of my leaving was my refusal to switch roles and lay my hands on anybody else. There was no question I would be asked to do for the two women what they had done for me.

I knew I could get away with walking out. And I did. It was selfish. It was self-centered. It was pretty much every flaw of mine on which my divorce was based and I keenly knew it. And still, I walked out. It's not an action I can justify these few hours later, nor likely ever, but it doesn't change my abandoning the group and the process. I just stayed there in that grass for two hours trying to will it all away.

I rejoined the group at lunch and everyone came up and hugged me. One woman complimented me on my bravery for walking out when I needed to walk out. Everyone complimented me on rejoining the group. If I hadn't been certified an asshole yet, this certainly clinched it, even if I was the only one who knew it. Although, now you know it too.

After lunch and an hour-long break to decompress the morning, Mary informed us that we would be ending the day with a trust walk.

Fuck me—a trust walk?

One of the most incorrect assumptions that people make about me is that I'm touchy-feely. I'm not. Yes, my background is in the professional cheerleading world of working in Student Affairs at various colleges and universities, but I have never fit the mold of said cheerleader. My biggest nightmare of an icebreaker is that demon-spawn "Human Knot" activity in which a group stands in a circle and you have to grab a hand of two different people with your two hands. Then, the whole group has to untangle the eponymous human knot until they are standing in one circle, hands still clasped together. My face inevitably ends up against someone's ass or my elbow on a breast, and sometimes those asses and breasts are those of students or a colleague with whom I have had difficulty. It's Twister without the alcohol, the social bonding, or the possibility of being a great first-date story for the grandkids. I really do like my space and any activities that have me both blindfolded and being led around just don't work for me.

Thus, this afternoon, when a purple scarf was tied around my head and one of my workshop peers led me around the Esalen grounds in silence for thirty minutes, it really was not in my comfort zone. It was thirty minutes of wandering around sightless in a strange land: on a grassy knoll situated on top of a towering cliff, with the sound of the waves crashing against the rocks, blinded by a scarf that clashed horribly with my ensemble. And, yes, my mind really went to that "Fashion Don't" place. But somewhere in those thirty minutes, I gave in and let myself be led around by an incredible partner who put fragrant leaves under my nose, pointed my face to the sun, put a stick in my hand, and had me bang some bells. It was a sensory nirvana and I reveled in the childlike wonder that coursed through the experience.

Far, far more difficult was when we switched roles and I was the leader. Based on my horrendous behavior earlier in the day, you would think that instead of physically leading this woman around, I would have just walked off, crumpling in some far-away grass as my blindfolded partner stumbled with outstretched arms toward the cliffs of Big Sur. But I stepped up.

Leading someone else around in that way, with their care placed so squarely in my charge, wasn't something I thought I needed, but ultimately, it was vital to my growth. In some small part, I needed to redeem myself for my abandonment of the group earlier in the day, even if that redemption was only happening in my own head. But, far more significantly, I needed to prove that I could shoulder the responsibility for someone else, that I could be there for another human being, and that I could suppress my ego and my selfishness to provide someone else with an experience that furthered their own development. It was an enormous responsibility and I embraced it.

Ultimately, it feels like today's tally tipped overwhelmingly toward the "Ken Failed" home team. But the opposing team got some points on the board at the end of the day, and I have to take a small bit of pride in that.

◆———————◆———————◆

Day 6
October 28, 2011

Somehow, already, today was our last day. It feels like we've been building up to something even if we just don't have the tools to describe what that something might be. Right from the start (after our last dance), Mary warned us that if we were expecting some sort of big bang, nuclear flash, moment of breakthrough, we were setting ourselves up for a gigantic disappointment. And yet, somehow, what I heard Mary say was that there would be some sort of big bang, nuclear flash, moment of breakthrough today. I'm a talented listener like that.

It's not that I didn't hear Mary's cautionary words. I just tossed them aside because I was so desperate for an emotional revelation that would yield answers to all of my questions:

Why do I sabotage everything that is so important to me?

How can I be a stalwart representative of ethics publically and then do everything contrary to my beliefs privately?

And, most important, how can I be reformed? Fixed? Made whole? Unbroken?

I heard Mary explicitly tell us not to expect answers, but surely it was okay for *me* to expect answers. Right?

This morning's exercises were a series of activities to get us comfortable with just sitting, really and truly sitting by ourselves, breathing serenely, and slowing things down. I would flunk a class in any one of those activities. Put all three together and it's almost a laughable pursuit for me. This week's break from technology was most certainly helpful in staying present and in the moment. But I also am feeling twitchy from not being able to respond to all of the emails that so unquestionably do not need my immediate attention but are still red-flagged as "High Importance." I most definitely worked through the activities this morning, but I couldn't get past the feeling that I'm just not that guy: I'm not the human who can easily disconnect or sit quietly just breathing or be by myself. I can certainly get better at all those things, but right this second they don't feel authentic.

After a ton of sitting and buckets of breathing serenely and oodles of slowing things down, we ate a quick lunch and then had an hour or so of free time before our last session together. As has happened pretty much every day, I was asked whether I wanted to take a dip in the mineral baths. As has not happened even once since I arrived here six days ago, I said yes.

This was revelatory for me on so many levels. First, I have always suffered from body dysmorphia. From being the scrawny kid in gym class to being the guy without defined abs in the gay community, I have never been comfortable walking around shirtless, much less fully nude. Second, you could count my experiences of being around naked women on one hand, and still come up with an accurate number if said hand had no fingers. There were no accidental incidents of walking in on my sisters, nor a regretted college encounter, or even mistakenly stumbling into a topless, lesbian rave (which may not be a thing, but clearly should be). So this prospect of immersing myself in the mineral baths with naked women I didn't know raised my anxiety level quite a bit.

And, of course, my fears were unfounded. Nobody cared about anyone else's body. Everyone was supportive of everyone else finding a spot in the tub. There was no ogling, no wolf-whistling, no lingering stares. It became yet another experience that I didn't know that I needed until I had it. Turns out that the mineral baths really were magical, imbued with gallons of healing properties. I soaked in the spirit with pores wide open.

After a quick shower and change of clothes it was time for our final session. Mary complimented us on our good work throughout the week and, as I looked around, it seemed like people really had made progress. People were sitting up straighter, bearing their scars more openly. There was a sense of confidence in the room that was far more palpable than it was when we first gathered together four days ago. Then I stopped looking around, cast my gaze inward, and just didn't see the progress. If I was going to make some leaps and bounds, I decided that I better throw myself into this last session. Procrastination at its finest.

Mary started out by talking about intention: that we really weren't the type of people who were able to coast through life without really thinking things through. She explained that she didn't mean that as a slight, but that, generally, the kind of people who sign up for her workshop are the kind of people who need more scaffolding and support as we move forward, at least for the time being. She then asked, "So what is your intention?" We all nodded. It was a deeply rhetorical question that set a tone of pondering as we settled in for our last session.

"No," Mary said after a minute or two of silence. "That wasn't a deeply rhetorical question to set a tone for our last session. Really, what is your intention? Here's a pen. Here's a piece of paper. Write it down."

So, what was my intention? What was it that I wanted out of all of this? What really was the goal in traveling *across the country* to be a part of an experience that, had I not felt broken, I never would have gone anywhere near? And, quick as that, there it was. With that last question the clouds parted, the angels started singing, and my intention was suddenly crystal clear.

Yes, I need to move forward emotionally. That was clear from the start of this journey. I need to not feel broken anymore, to be able to feel whole, to be able to walk around Brattleboro, Vermont, without freaking out because a blue Yaris passed me on the street. But that was decided before I even got on a plane to come to California.

The light bulb moment came from my reflecting that I had indeed traveled across the country to find the answers. Yes, I thought that Esalen would help me, but implicit in that belief was the absolute certainty that help was not going to be found in Brattleboro. It was significant that the thought had never crossed my mind that there was something I could do in

Vermont to become whole again, certainly not when I was too busy scanning the parking lot of the award-winning farmers' market for that blue Yaris first before parking my own car to pick up those locally-sourced beets. I realized in that moment not only was I broken, but so too was Vermont. There was nothing left for me in Vermont and it was a place where I would never be able to heal.

Now, I'm no fool. I know that issues of the heart tend to not recognize state lines. But I also knew with 100 percent certainty that I needed a kick in the ass as much with my physical location as with my mental state if I ever hoped to heal. Thus I gripped that pen and wrote in big bold letters: Intention: to move forward to the next phase of my life emotionally *and* geographically

It felt great. It felt right. It felt like it was a step in a healthy direction.

Mary then explained that an intention was nothing without a plan: an actual concrete plan with steps and dates attached to it. How were we going to get to where we needed to go? What were the discrete actions that we could take to fulfill what we just wrote down? In short, what would we actually *do*?

Having spent so many months wandering around in a fog, I didn't think coming up with action steps would be an easy task. There have certainly been moments recently when the desire to dig myself out of the hole was overpowering. But in each of those moments, the blurriness made action feel unreachable. In that moment, this afternoon in that room at Esalen, my now-articulated intention cut through the fog with ease. My plan actually started to come together pretty quickly and once I started writing, there was no turning back.

Step 1: Stop contacting my ex-husband, including checking his Facebook page. Yes, in my head, I understand that a divorce means not being together. But somehow this has never translated into a lessening of my reaching out. And not just reaching out, but reaching out about stupid stuff, like, "Hey, do you know where that thing is that I don't really care about but I still get to email you to establish contact to inquire about the whereabouts of the thing about which I don't really care?" And, if I wasn't sending him emails, I was checking his Facebook page many, many times throughout the day. I was desperately searching for some sort of glimpse that he felt broken too. This behavior is not helping me. *Timeline for Step 1: Immediately*

Step 2: Job hunt like a crazy person. There are so many positions in higher education out there in the world, and only 2 percent of them are in Vermont. I need to aggressively chase the other 98 percent that are in places distinctly not Vermont. *Timeline for Step 2: Immediately. Either finish out the school year and set up shop with my folks in New Jersey or leave Vermont as soon as I find a new job.*

Step 3: No work email at home. In the scheme of things, this didn't feel like a major step. But there was so much drama in my daily life with campus alcohol and other drug issues, sexual misconduct, the deterioration of students' mental health, and helicopter parents that I could never truly embrace Step 2 if I didn't start establishing boundaries here in Step 3. *Timeline for Step 3: Immediately.*

Step 4: Attend the local salon night. There is a wonderful author named Suzanne Kingsbury who lives in Brattleboro and organizes a monthly writing salon for people to sit around, munch on cheese and crackers, and write and share their scribbles. I so desperately need a creative outlet as a pressure release valve, and I enjoyed myself there that one time I attended the salon a few years back. It's time to aggressively pursue the things that actually bring me joy. *Timeline for Step 4: Attend the November Salon Gathering.*

Step 5: Forgive myself. Yeah. So there's that. *Timeline for Step 5: Ongoing.*

I'm not fooling myself to think that my life is going to change dramatically due to the process of writing an intention and a few action steps, but each pen-stroke felt like a pinprick of awareness that poked through my opaque blanket of hurt. I felt a little bit more light cut through the blurriness after having written all this down. I relayed this sentiment to Mary and she really and truly said, "Did I not tell you to listen to me, dumbass?"

The rest of the day post-dumbass was not all that memorable. All I could think about was that I now had a piece of paper with a plan. It was the most important piece of paper in my world and I was excited to make those words jump off the page and into my life. This dumbass could make things happen.

Day 7
October 29, 2011

Is change possible? Or is change a farce we buy into until the circumstances around us thrust us into another landscape, convincing us that we have changed when, in fact, it was the details that changed and not us? The delta in word count between these first and second sentences gives slight indication as to which way my scales are tilting, but I still feel that overwhelming persuasion that change is possible, even as I sit here riddled with doubt.

Doubt is a crazy thing, given that I put so much stock in an individual's capacity to change society. Heck, that's what I actually spend my days trying to teach college students. But substantive and lasting change that takes root in an individual? I have tried to stay pretty far away from that question and even farther away when the individual in question is me. If there's some irony in the idea that I believe more in the capacity to change an entire social system than I do in the ability to change a single individual, it is an irony that I can only barely sense. This is not to say that this week hasn't challenged me; that, at least, is not in question. I have unquestionably learned that the only way that I am going to move forward is if I first believe something is amiss ("I am broken") and then have the desire to change it (*see: Ken's intention*).

This last morning at Esalen was predictably emotional. We hugged. We complimented each other. We wished each other great health. I have spent the past five-plus days doing intense work for eight to ten hours a day in the same small room with the same small group. A cocoon had formed around this makeshift family ("as opposed to your relatives," Mary repeatedly highlighted) and the idea of leaving and returning to Vermont was daunting. At one point, I expressed concern about departing from the cliffs of Esalen and Mary quickly interjected, "Are you walking out right now?

With hours left to go, I replied, "No."

"Then you're not leaving yet and there's no reason to put yourself in that future," she responded. We both knew that her advice applied to far more than my imminent trip home. My almost-complete inability to live in the present is something I have always known. This week has helped me see that the past really is unalterable and my desire to change it only throws me back to the Land of the Broken. The next step forward will be to have at least one foot dangling in the kiddie pool of the present as opposed to my entire body submerged in the twin oceans of the past and future.

Before we said our last good-byes, Mary asked us once again to pull out that piece of paper with our intentions and our action steps. As I had already been gripping that paper in my hand, it took me perhaps the shortest amount of time to produce the document. She asked us to read it to ourselves one more time and pay particular attention to the timeline. She predicted that the majority of steps on our action plan could be accomplished immediately. That reality slammed into me in a way that didn't register when I penned those words yesterday.

Most of my actions could be accomplished with a mouse click as opposed to struggling through processes "...spread out over decades. I had originally thought that the latter would always trump the former on this path and that the importance of clicking "Block" on Facebook would pale in importance next to some deep-rooted soul work. But reading that list this morning made it clear that action is action. Assigning weight and meaning to this footstep over that one denies the full value of moving forward. It was an empowering new reality.

And then, just like that, our workshop was over. It was time to say our good-byes. Tears, laughter, and wistfulness abounded. These were not my people; our lives were so disconnected. These were also incontestably my people; we all had our work to do. It was difficult to leave them behind.

I actually had previously signed up for an additional two-and-a-half-day workshop on meditation practices, but the idea of being with a different group of people felt wrong, so I went straight to the front desk to ask whether I could both back out and receive a refund. It was clear that I was not the first person to change his mind at the last minute about a workshop. The Esalen staff quickly let me back out of the additional two-and-a-half days.

With an unchangeable flight two-and-a-half days away, this then gave me sixty hours to spend in Monterey, California, with absolutely no plan in front of me. In an unbelievable stroke of good fortune, Gina, the fellow workshop participant with whom I most closely bonded, had the same extra time built into her trip. So we spent a solid few days walking around, seeing the sights, and processing anything that crossed our paths.

We went to the Monterey Bay Aquarium and had the most fantastic time ever. Had you asked me last week about my enthusiasm level for aquariums, I would have immediately replied with a resounding "Meh." But the Monterey Bay Aquarium completely blew my mind. Everything was a metaphor: the penguins in California, the endangered sea otters, and the fish that kept swimming around and around.

We went to the movies to see whatever was playing. The only movie that fit into our schedule was *The Way*. Had you asked me last week about my enthusiasm level for a movie about Martin Sheen walking the Camino de Santiago to honor his dead son, I would have immediately replied with a resounding "Meh." But *The Way* completely blew my mind. Everything was a metaphor: grieving an irreparable loss, meeting supportive strangers along your path forward, and everyone yelling "Buen Camino" at you, wishing you a "Good Walk" as you take step after step toward your destination.

We spent a good chunk of time sitting on benches looking out at Monterey Bay. Had you asked me last week about my enthusiasm level for sitting on a bench without electronics just looking out at the water, I would have immediately replied with a resounding "Meh." But sitting on that bench completely blew my mind. Everything was a metaphor: the unending waves rolling in and out, the stream of disconnected people walking by us, and yes, those sea lions out there on the rock in front of us. My obsession with figuring out those sea lions was reaching epic and distracting proportions. They held the key to my healing and I felt like I was right there on the verge of firmly grasping their meaning in my life.

Sadly, those sixty hours flew by, and it was time for Gina and I to say our good-byes. So here I sit in my hotel room before I need to head out to the airport in a few hours. I can't help but try to decipher what it was that I had actually learned here in California. Am I still broken? Was I different pre- and post-Esalen? What did I now know that I didn't a week ago?

I certainly know more about the way I respond to situations and my own Defenses. Mary had repeatedly said that even if you don't respond to situations differently, you will never look at your responses the same way again. I already have proof that that assertion is true. The Intellectualizer, The Perfectionist, and The Entertainer have all been named, and with faces attached to their wily ways, I think I can do a far better job at actively minimizing their dominance over the way I react.

I now know that I'm not alone. It seems like such a simple and trite realization, but a combination of ego and hiding my true pain often results in me thinking, "I'm the only one out here feeling broken and, sure, I can let people know that I'm hurting, but only the surface-level pain, not the real stuff." It definitely took some hardcore prodding from Mary and the structure of a healing workshop on the other side of the country, but I walk away from this experience knowing that there really are folks who can support you and, perhaps even more important, need your support in return.

And, although this last one is going to take a lot of reminders, I now know that contemplating that which has not yet happened is a luxury of an individual who knows with 100 percent certainty that he will be there to experience that which has not yet happened. Or, more succinctly, I need to be more present. It's one thing when you walk away with this revelation after a screening of *Dead Poet's Society* and buy the *"Carpe Diem"* t-shirt at American Apparel. It is quite another thing when you connect this future-gazing to current pain.

Again, I am not so delusional as to think I could be remade in five days in a foreign land. I am still me. The Defenses are still there. The pain hasn't gone away. I am indeed still feeling broken. But I also am not so jaded that I am unable to recognize that this time away has been a gift, an opportunity for growth, and a privilege afforded to a select few. To refuse that gift, to not acknowledge that opportunity, and to deny that privilege would all be to say that I don't want change. And I do. I actually am closer to thinking that change is possible, not only just for me but also for anyone who needs the idea of change. There's still so much for us all to do! Not that I'm looking to the future—I promised I wouldn't.

Ok, I am.

I am looking to the future.

But I'm doing so with eyes wide open on where I am right this very second. And that's not nothing. In fact, it almost feels like something.

As for the parable of the sea lions, it turns out they really were symbolic.

I watched them for days in Monterey, post-Esalen, trying to discern their meaning in my journey. Was it my Odyssean voyage through the "sea?" My Tarzanian quest to be the "lion" on land? Or perhaps my attempt to live the contradiction between the different realms of sea and land?

At my last meal here in Monterey a few hours ago, I dined at a local restaurant that was situated on a pier a few feet away from a huge rock with dozens of sea lions staring right into my soul. I was convinced they were actively willing me forward into a future where I embraced my pain and overcame it. I asked my waiter how those sea lions relate to one another and the world, and even as the question left my mouth, I knew that this lanky eighteen-year old with his desperate and unsuccessful attempt to grow facial hair was my Athena. He knew these sea lions. He basked in their energy all day long. He, and he alone, knew their symbolism and thus held the answer to all the meaning of this work in my life.

"Huh?" he asked, I assumed, in an attempt to really harness both the spirit of my question and the spirit of the sea lions. I repeated my query to elicit his sea lion Celestine Prophecy.

"Oh," my sage waiter replied. He paused and looked out to the rock, gathering his chi as he delivered that which would provide the divination that would direct all my days to come. I knew in that moment that I was the sea lion and in seconds, this oracle would tell me why.

"Yeah, dude, those aren't sea lions. Those are harbor seals. They just sit around, sleep, shit, and bark when something gets in their way. Plus, they eat a lot of garbage and we all hate them. Did you want dessert?"

As the sea lions and the blurriness faded from my life, I knew that yes, yes I did.

I did want dessert.

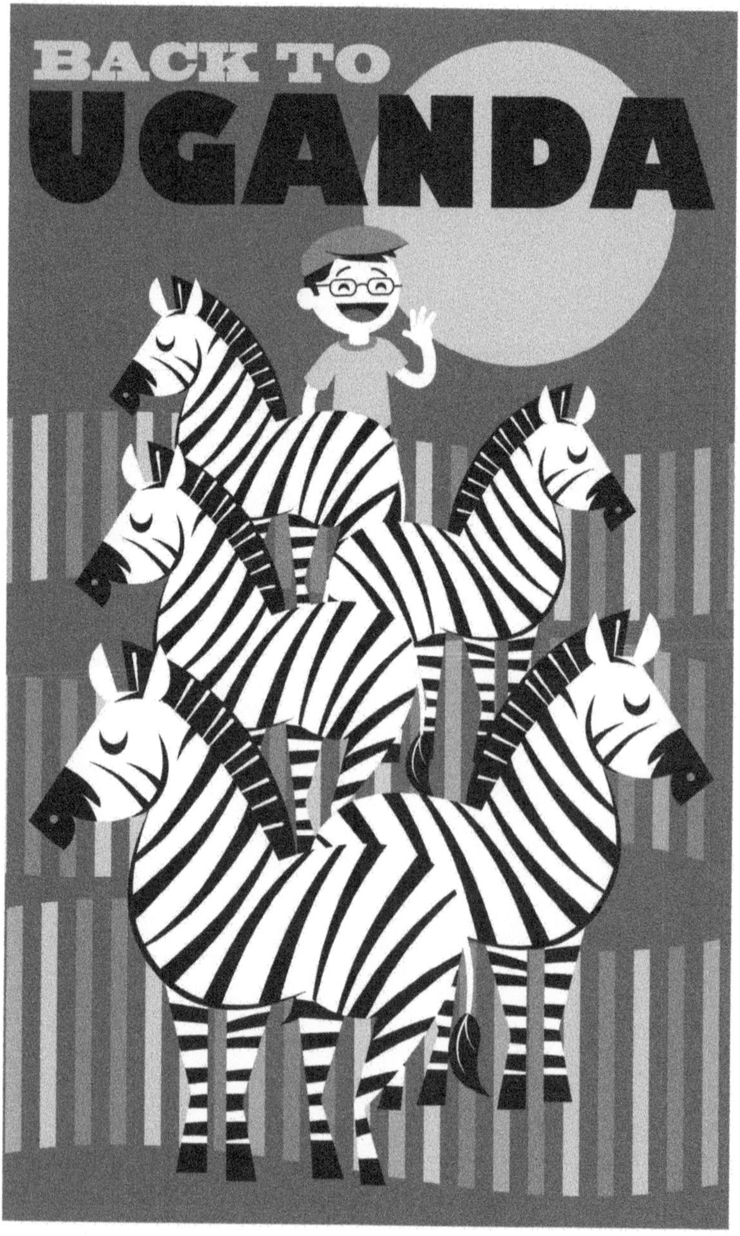
BACK TO
UGANDA

Uganda Strikes Back

(Uganda: November 15, 2012 – November 23, 2012)

Days 1, 2 & 3
November 15–17, 2012

> *Tulibalu-GANDA.*
> *TU-libaluganda.*
> *Tu-LI-baluganda.*

N o matter how you pronounce it, it still sounds like a total crock of shit.

Not the concept, mind you. The idea that there is some sort of universal truth that binds together souls in a partnership of pure fellowship, well, who can fault that? A six-syllable word that roughly translates to "We are all brethren" should be a game-changer, an epithet with the ability to stop conflict and induce peace wherever and whenever it is verbally brandished. But to use the phrase as I did two years ago as a trite, pithy summary to somehow resolve all of the conflict in my head, well that, THAT is a crock of shit.

I needed a trite, pithy summary back then. I was just so overwhelmed by it all: by Gloria, by Uganda, by being out in the world in a wholly different way than I had ever been before in my life. I keenly knew there was so much more to write, but the feeling of being overwhelmed rushed my pen toward a tidy ending so that I could end that chapter and feel a sense of closure as quickly as I could, however artificial.

I was left with so many questions but I needed more time to get the answers. When I returned home and read what I had written, it was clear to me that I didn't just need more time in my own head, I needed more time in Uganda, more time at Busingye School, and even more time with Gran Gloria.

And so, amazingly, here I sit, two years and some change later, back in the self-described pearl of Africa in a hotel room near the airport in Entebbe. Entebbe in Uganda. Uganda in Africa.

It should follow that there is a ton of backstory between Uganda Act 1 and this Uganda Act 2, but there is surprisingly little for me to report. I spent a month in China this summer with a group of students. While there, I thought, "Hey, now *that* was a long flight to China. You know what else was a long flight? The flight to Uganda. I should go back there." On rare occasions, my thought process really is that linear. And that was the totality of my thinking.

Although the decision to return was not terribly complex, you should not assume my life has followed a linear path. Because, seriously, it so has not. I'm not the same person I was two years ago. I'm not *even* sure I'm the same species. Let us count the differences.

The first change is with this journal. I write now knowing it will be read. From me, to you. Something clicked midway through penning my first Ugandan experiences when I suddenly knew I wasn't just writing for me. I didn't quite know exactly who the reader was going to be, but I knew my journey was slightly bigger than me.

I took that first Uganda journal with me on stage a few times and read those words aloud to a few hundred folks with accompanying photos I had snapped. As well-received as my musings seemed to have been, the post-reading Q&As revealed an audience's need for more: they wanted more about the experience of gay people in Uganda, more about the complexities of Gloria, and more about how my experiences affected the way I see both myself and the world around me. The audience's needs helped me articulate my own needs. And those needs are a huge source of motivation for me this second time around.

The second change is with this trip itself. It surprised my friends and family that I decided to return to Uganda via Gloria. For me, this was a no-brainer. I needed a comparative experience and I wanted the umbrella of safety that her trip provides through the well-worn journey she executes four times a year.

That said, the composition, timing, and purpose of this trip are entirely different than my first go-round. The group of thirteen is now five: Gran Gloria, her son, a young PR dude, me, and another woman named Gloria. No joke. Because that's what I thought I was missing . . . a second Gloria. The August, nine-day, mug

123

shot-taking trip is now seven days in November with the purpose of throwing a schoolwide Christmas party. Again: in November. Even I, the gay Jew from New Jersey, know that we're off by a few weeks, but we brought packets of Skittles and sunglasses for all thousand-plus children so Father Noël can surely be given a pass for starting his gift-giving journey in Uganda a month early.

The third and last change will undoubtedly affect the words on the pages ahead far more than the other two changes. That change would be me. Two years ago, I was married and three weeks away from adopting a baby from Phoenix, the place where I learned the stork drops all available babies. Now, I'm divorced and am the caretaker for a cat who just barely tolerates me. Barely. And only because I fill his bowl with food each day.

Two years ago, I was fully entrenched as a dean of students and was completely faithful to my field of student affairs. Now, I gave my notice a few weeks ago and have seven months left to figure out what I'm going to do with the rest of my life. At the time of this writing, my next vocation is either going to be (a) teaching, or (b) opening up a small eatery in Vermont named "Mush," where I would serve my world-famous stew-like mush in an establishment about which top food critics would call, "Quaint, quirky, queer, and quasi-life-changing. Dive into the Mush. You won't regret it."

Two years ago, I traveled to Uganda having just finished my immersion in AIDS/LifeCycle surrounded by the most amazing gay people and allies who loved and supported me unconditionally. Now, I just finished reading a text message from the last guy left to date in Southern Vermont who was breaking up with me via pixel because he found the woman—the woman!— of his dreams as they reached for the same beet at the farmers' market. And yes, you read that correctly. Go on ahead and read that one again. I'll wait.

Two years ago, I stood on solid ground. Now, I'm immersed in this transitional phase, a time most beloved by those who aren't on solid ground and need to make this lack of stability sound like something distinctly more appealing.

The only thing I know for sure about my new self, the one piece to which I am firmly clinging, is that my new lens is going to alter my approach. I firmly believe these changes will help me both ask better questions and maybe—maybe—get some answers. While I can't control the latter, the former has inspired a great big list of questions.

I want to ask Gloria about her juxtaposition of brash, American corporate culture on this school in rural Uganda. I want to ask Nurse Liana about what guides her on this path to provide care in the way that she does. I want to ask *Musamesa* Gilbert about how he teaches in that incredible way I witnessed. I want to ask the children about their hopes. I want to ask the headmaster why he chose *Mutebi* for me. And I want to ask someone, and hopefully a lot of someones, about the "Kill the Gays" legislation. Last week, the Ugandan Parliament downgraded the punishment for being gay to lifetime imprisonment, which is slightly less harsh than execution, but is still not exactly a welcome atmosphere for all the gays because, y'know, imprisonment.

I chickened out my first time here and didn't ask the questions that were in my head. It's not that I didn't want to learn more, I just didn't have solid footing to get the information I needed. This time around, I'm ready to be more proactive. If I actually ask all of those questions of all of those people, I should get a ton of answers. That's how this works, right? Because I really am hoping that's how this works.

With regard to my travel over these past two days, there isn't too much to report other than it still takes a colossal amount of time to get to Uganda. I drove four-and-a-half hours from Vermont to Gloria's house in New Jersey. Then it was the plane part of the trip: a three-and-a-half-hour wait in Newark, a six-and-a-half-hour flight to Amsterdam, a two-and-a-half-hour wait on the tarmac on that plane in Amsterdam, an eight-hour flight to Rwanda, and one more hour-long flight to Uganda. I left Vermont at 9:30 a.m. on a Thursday, and it is now almost midnight on Friday. I *think* in the same year, but my body is not entirely convinced. Needless to say, I am tired and about to head to bed.

I should note that greeting Gloria again was very complex and Vidalia-onion-layered for me. We immediately embraced and she seemed genuinely happy to see me, which clearly meant that she had blessedly not heard a word I wrote about her two years ago. I was then suddenly and completely overcome with guilt because I felt like I ultimately trashed her in my previous writings. There she was this afternoon: a humanitarian who was showing me the thousands of bags of candy she had secured to enhance the children's Christmas celebrations. Anything I had previously written that cast her in a negative light now felt positively unjust.

Then, Gloria said something sharply and oh-so-painfully critical of someone who worked at the Busingye School. In her next breath, she joyously told me that she has raised enough money to buy each child—all thousand-plus of them—a brand new outfit, something most of their families simply could not afford and something their peers across the country would never experience. Then she said something else sharply and oh-so-painfully critical about someone else and I suddenly remembered, "Oh, yeah. This whole situation is complex. So too is this woman."

And regarding that woman, I really want to figure her out this time around.

I fall asleep now clutching a wriggling and slippery tendril of hope that I can find some real answers my second time here in Uganda. I'm holding on tight to that hope. I'm a different person now and I'm ready for a different experience. Ready and willing. All that's left to figure out is the able.

Day 4
November 18, 2012

I woke up tired. Bone-weary tired.

At breakfast, my tripmates all spoke of fitful nights of sleep, whereas my lover, Baron Benedict Benadryl, and I slept limbs intertwined right through the night. Even so, I emerged under a veil of grogginess. Thankfully, the daily itinerary set in front of us didn't look particularly demanding. We popped down to the lobby for a quick bite to eat. I discovered that Pineapple 2012 didn't taste quite as mind-blowing as Pineapple 2010, but I confirmed that Nutella is just as sun-kissed by God in Uganda as it is the whole world 'round. We then piled into our Land Cruiser to start the three-hour ride to the Equator. On the ride, a few observations immediately came to light.

> **Observation #1:** Our seven-person vehicle was infinitely more comfortable than the fifteen-passenger sardine can we crammed into two years ago. Here, there was some physical and emotional breathing room. With the previous group of fifteen, I remember us often breaking into smaller subgroups, but with this group of five, I really could observe what everyone else was experiencing. This led to Observation #2.
>
> **Observation #2:** I'm feeling a little "too cool for school" right now. I'm just not as wide-eyed as my peers who were witnessing Uganda for the first time. The winner-takes-all open-course streets in which only the most aggressive driver wins? Seen 'em. The ramshackle living sheds garishly painted on the outside by cell phone companies and beverage conglomerates? Seen 'em. Bags of grasshoppers being sold by the side of the road for human consumption? Seen 'em and still zero inclination to try 'em. I certainly was not intending to be blasé about everything foreign before me nor did I wish to take even a second of it for granted. But I was feeling a bit blasé about everything foreign before me and was most definitely taking a multitude of things for granted.

Two hours later, we arrived at the Equator and my little two-year old friend was nowhere in sight. It was silly to be disappointed to not see a boy who doubtlessly would not remember the

American from two-and-a-half years ago, but I was disappointed. This was the first comparative experience I was going to have and I had to put it aside. What else was going to be different? Did the country of Uganda and her people not know I was coming back?

I realized last night that I left my journal in Amsterdam—which is both true and fun to write—so I wandered into a paper-shop to buy a new one. With this first purchase of the trip, I was immediately reminded of both the practice of haggling as well as my supreme discomfort with the practice of haggling. In 2010, one of my tripmates had always helped me with haggling, by which I mean, I would select an item, throw money at my trip-mate, run away from the location of the sale, and later get my item and more change than I had anticipated from my haggling knight.

This time, I was on my own.

I selected my journal and brought it to the counter. The saleslady quietly told me it was twenty thousand shillings. I boldly countered with seventeen thousand shillings. I then looked in my wallet and saw that I only had fifteen thousand shillings. So I boldly countered my own offer with fifteen thousand shillings. The saleslady paused, whispered okay, and—I might be wrong about this—looked at me with a little disappointment. In turn—and I'm definitely not wrong about this—I felt like crap. I thought haggling was supposed to be a fun game in which both parties emerged smiling from their joint negotiating adventure. Instead, my victory in haggling dissipated immediately in the face of the reality that I had only saved two dollars. Economics being what they are, this also meant I had denied someone else two dollars. And knowing what I know about the economy of this region, that two dollars likely meant more to the saleslady than it did to me. Head bowed, I quickly slithered out of the shop.

After a brief snack of chapati chips and guacamole, we piled back into the van for the last traffic-filled hour on the way to the hotel. The funny thing about traffic is that it makes your vehicle slow down. In some cases, when the traffic is particu-larly congested, it can even make your vehicle stop. In this case, the immense amounts of traffic made our vehicle stop for long stretches of time. An annoyance for us? Slightly. An unbelievably exciting opportunity for children to see the crazy *mazungas* (white people)? Enormously.

Here's how it repeatedly went down. Our vehicle stops. Children see us. They go nuts and lose their shit. They wave their arms and shout, "*Mazunga! Mazunga!*" Now, I really do mean that they lose their shit. They brighten. They jump up and down. They jockey with other bouncing groupies to get a better position out front.

The best I can understand this fangirling is that it's essentially like seeing a unicorn. You mostly don't see unicorns, right? But if and when you were to see a unicorn, you would most certainly go nuts. The unicorn is a symbol of exotic fantasy and untapped prosperity. And the unicorn-spotting would be an unbelievable source of validation should the unicorn look your way. Further, should that unicorn whip out a camera—and I know I have officially taken this analogy too far—but, yes, should that unicorn whip out a camera and want to take a picture of *you*, well you would go nuts and lose your shit. Thus, because it was all so humbling and flattering and because our group was keenly aware that we were providing excitement, we never failed to whip out our cameras and take pictures of the children.

We eventually arrived at the hotel in Masaka, dumped our items in the lobby, and set off back to Otuzzi, the cooperative village we visited two years ago. The road leading to the village was just as insane, albeit slightly more bearable given our smaller vehicle. I opted out of the tour of Otuzzi that was offered to our group. I knew the tour would ultimately lead to the dentist's office and that run-down dentist's chair for which I never even made one call to replace. I wasn't ready to look that chair in the eyes.

I busied myself by reading a hand-lettered poster explaining the mission of the village and kept returning to the last sentence, "Otuzzi attempts to not work on a policy of charity but on increasing the capacity of the surrounding community."

Increasing the capacity of the surrounding community. There's a nugget of gold in there somewhere I really want to mine with my civic pickaxe when I return to America. I also wondered how much Gran Gloria jived with this philosophy but I wasn't ready to look that humanitarian in the eye.

The village of Otuzzi now sports gardening plots for the villagers. Instead of numbering or lettering them, the plots have been named after random counties. This practice was made all the more intriguing given that this village is the very definition of remote. Very few of the residents will ever have the opportunity to leave their neighborhood, much less central Uganda, much less Africa, and, certainly, much less go to Thailand and Egypt. The signs felt aspirational if unrealistic.

Also, today we met an insanely adorable Jewish Canadian playwright staying in Otuzzi for the month and he kept adorably using the phrase, "Good on ya!" to the point where I kept trying to not-so-adorably slip my accomplishments into our conversation so I could earn another of his, "Good on ya!"s. I was obvious and relentless, but that's how great each "Good on ya" made me feel.

I hereby resolve to use "Good on ya!" more in my daily parlance so, good on ya for reading these words, and good on ya for being invested in my adventures, and good on ya for recommending this book to everyone you have ever encountered in life. And please don't think that I'm not disappointed that it doesn't look as adorable in writing or when I speak it aloud. Ah well. Quick dinner ahead and then off to bed before it's back to that Pentecostal church in the morning.

Good on ya, Jesus!

◆———————◆———————◆

Day 5
November 19, 2012

I woke up groggy again today, which seems ridiculous given that Baron Benadryl and I spooned for a full ten hours of uninterrupted slumber. And my throat felt a little bit sore, which I thought meant I either had contracted malaria or that I was minimally dehydrated. After downing some bottled water, I was able to quickly confirm that it was the latter malady.

After breakfast, it was time to return to church for Sunday worship. I keenly remember penning the words two years ago that attending a Pentecostal church service in Uganda was a once-in-a-lifetime experience, so I was really excited to take in the whole service this morning with my experienced and appreciative eyes. Zealot prophets that we were, we arrived at the church a bit early, so we detoured quickly to Busingye Advanced Day and Boarding Primary School to drop off supplies for the goodie bags for the Christmas party.

We were immediately greeted by Joseph, the headmaster, and Ibrahim, the assistant headmaster (he of flex arms, growling *"Mutebi!"* fame). As soon as I stepped out of that Land Cruiser, they yelled *"Musamesa* Ken" and embraced me warmly. That honorific of *"Musamesa,"* (teacher), well, I'm not sure I can fully express how much it made me puff up with pride. It felt like more than an acknowledgment of my vocation; somewhere in those four syllables, I felt a kinship and, using my most academic, *Musamesa*-y vocabulary, it rocked.

After a quick unload of tchotchkes and Gloria sternly telling us that we didn't have time to dilly-dally, we headed back to the church. The service was in full swing when we arrived and we were once again escorted to the sacred white plastic lawn chairs. At this point, I have to assume Jesus and his apostles lounged on those plastic thrones somewhere in that newer testament that I was taught neither at Temple Emanuel in Woodcliff Lake, New Jersey, nor have ever read on my own. To be seated on those chairs again was an honor. Truly.

There were a dozen or so songs, a millennia or two of prayers, and then, surprise! there was a theater experience! And not just theater, but youth theater! Now this was a treat. A group of children put on quite the eye-opening play in honor of the "Dear American Visitors," a phrase I had forgotten and still very much disliked. From what I understood of the plot—a process made difficult by the single decibel, crackling sound system—there was a group of three supplicants who had no money. They repeatedly sought out financial assistance from a rich man who kept turning down their requests.

Those three supplicants then sought help from a generous man who, as it turns out, was extraordinarily generous to a life-altering fault. The generous man gave funds to the first supplicant, then doled out funds to the second supplicant, and was *just* about to finish spreading his wealth to the third supplicant when, <gasp!>, he dropped dead. Like actually dropped dead to the floor. Seriously, I did a quick intake of breath as I didn't actually see that plot twist coming. Thankfully, the third supplicant was able to get in touch with Jesus Christ. (Side note: the other two supplicants walked right offstage, content with the coin they had already banked). Jesus then addressed the audience, via fake telephone, that we must all be more generous.

Jesus then set out to resurrect the generous man. Because Jesus can do that, I think? Here's the thing: we don't actually know whether the resurrection was truly successful because the children started singing a song as the generous man's corpse was escorted offstage. But let's go ahead and assume it was indeed a successful revival. Because we're all more comfortable with that outcome, right? An unsuccessful Jesus is a completely different version of youth theater and one that didn't seem to fit into this church's world view.

The rest of the service was long. Like holy cow, really long. The sermon this time around was all about repenting, and, by the end, I didn't feel so bad about skipping the Jewish High Holiday services this year. Attending this service and sermon more than makes up for my absence. Agreed, Mom?

At one point, we were called up to introduce ourselves to the congregation. Just as Gloria had not told us two years ago that we would have to stand up front and perform this task, so too did I omit this detail to my two tripmates who were experiencing all the pentecosting for the first time. Was this a form of Ugandan hazing? Sure. But I folded any attendant guilt I may have had into the sermon on repentance I had just endured. I felt washed clean.

I was an old pro at this, a well-experienced hand at Pentecostal platitudes. Let's see. What word could I throw out to the congregation to win everyone over? What six syllables would sway the hearts of these faith-attuned Ugandans assembled before me? What could it be?

No sooner did I finish the "da" in *"Tulibaluganda"* than the audience expressed a collective "oooh!" and started clapping. I was fairly sure that if Jesus wasn't successful in his task a few minutes before, my utterance most assuredly brought the generous man back to his original vitality, much to the pleasure of both the congregation and the third supplicant who was still looking for cash.

There were, again, countless moments of religious devotion and faith writ large across the faces of those around me. I stared openly at the congregants, from the oldest, stooped parishioner to the three-year old boy on my right, on his knees, scrunching up his face and praying hard to his heavenly father. I was, again, marginally jealous that I had not connected to a faith with even the tiniest fraction of this three-year old's fervency. But I also accepted that fact as I had no idea how such a fervency could fit into my life.

After the service had concluded, a supremely wizened congregant approached me outside the church talking animatedly. Someone else translated that she was in total shock and awe as she had never seen a white person at a born again church in her many, many years. She was so appreciative of Jesus for my spiritual journey, so much so that I swallowed down the words "gay" and "Jew" right quick. I asked whether we could take a picture together and she replied that she would be honored. She then hilariously tossed her walking stick aside lest she be holding a prop that would make her look anything other than spry. I couldn't stop smiling as we re-boarded our vehicle.

After the service, we set out to finish our day at the school. I sadly learned that *Musamesa* Gilbert had moved on to teach at a university. I was disappointed. This was the second comparative experience I was going to have and I had to put it aside. What else was going to be different? Did the country of Uganda and her people not know I was coming back?

Musawu (Nurse) Liana was indeed still working there, most certainly not fired, and she and I embraced warmly. She asked how my wife and baby were doing. I responded that I really liked what she had done with her hair. It was a code that was clear... well, to me at least.

Today's task put out in front of us at the school was simple: assemble and stuff eleven hundred goodie bags complete with plastic sunglasses, a bouncy ball, a creepy googly-eye ring, a kazoo, a few stickers, a string of plastic Mardi Gras beads, and many, many pieces of candy. That candy felt like a total slap in the face to Toothbrush-palooza 2010, but I kept that irony to myself. Packing the bags was slow work but we made a ton of progress, finishing 510 bags over the span of a few hours.

At various points during our assembly line process, Gran Gloria barked various orders. There wasn't a lot of room to make a mistake here as we just needed to put the things from the one table in the bags on the other table, so her instructions felt pretty inane and all kinds of moot. Now seventy-five, Gloria was just as forceful and caustic as ever. This was a woman who wanted things done in a certain way and had no hesitation about letting you know exactly how that way should look.

Anytime someone at the school asked her how she was doing, she seemed obsessed with responding to every inquiry by detailing her seventeen nightmarish days after Hurricane Sandy when she was without power in New Jersey. And every Ugandan who heard this tale fell over backwards, telling her how horrible that must have been for her and how grateful to God they were that she survived.

That she survived!

Never mind that those seventeen nightmarish days of sporadic electricity were the baseline here in Uganda. They were so happy that she survived. And I couldn't shake the feeling that I was right back in that place of confusion and uncertainty where I ended on that last day two years ago. Here we were organizing thousands of bags of crap, which *might* be appreciated for a $2.18 value on *Antique's Roadshow*. But it was $2.18 worth of crap that genuinely pleases the children and $2.18 worth of crap that really and truly separated these students by a moat of temporary privilege from the children on the other side of the school walls. With the joy that is about to be created through this $2.18 worth of crap, does the delivery vessel really matter? Does the style truly affect the inevitably joyous outcome? On a greater scale, with the medical coverage and assistance that Gloria provides, should I care about the process (Gloria's no-nonsense behavior) given the product (Gloria's successful outcomes)?

We took a break from bag stuffing and I needed a few minutes away from that assembly line and Gloria's continuous retelling of her stint on *Survivor: New Jersey*. I left the assembly line and wandered into an instructional class of P2, the equivalent of first grade. I was joined by Linda, the other assistant headmaster. I made some inane off-the-cuff comment—y'know, as I do—saying something like, "Oh how I would love to teach here." To which Linda replied, "So teach. Class, this is *Musamesa* Ken. Listen to him." Mind you, I had an almost identical experience of being suddenly given control of a foreign class in China a few months ago and, there, I knocked my adjunct lecturer role out of the ballpark.

Here in Uganda, however, I froze. I have no clue what happened. The academic topic for the day was math, admittedly not my strong suit, but I thought I could pull off first grade instruction. I couldn't. I babbled. Linda helped a little. I babbled some more. I eventually stopped and thanked them. Linda said, "You should come back and teach here if you ever leave your job at the university." I replied, "I actually am leaving my university job in May." She concluded, "Then you should come back here and teach in May." And somewhere in that rapid-fire exchange, a seed was planted.

Look, I'm impulsive. I know that. Compulsive too. And I know that too. But in seven months, I will have no job and no real reason to stay in either Vermont or even in the United States. Why not teach in Uganda for a year? It was certainly something to ponder.

We were able to finish another three hundred bags, bringing our total to 810 bags and it was time to leave for the day. We were headed to 10 Tables, the most upscale restaurant in all of Kampala and we were informed by our Canadian dinnermates, Bridget and Bruce, that we were going to be joined by the U.S. Ambassador to Uganda.

Really?

Cool!

Bridget and Bruce are two of the most incredible people I have ever encountered on this planet. They have lived in Uganda for decades, with a brief break in the 1970s when Idi Amin personally kicked them out, y'know, as he did. Bruce farms pineapples in Otuzzi and Bridget volunteers forty hours a week as a maternity nurse at a hospital in Kampala, having been the nurse in the village of Otuzzi for years. She was the woman who had originally showed me that dentist's chair. Needless to say, I was really excited to be breaking bread tonight with Bridget and Bruce.

In the ride over to the restaurant, Gloria was rehearsing her speech for the ambassador. It went something like this: "Hello. My name is Gloria Thomas. I run Gloria's Children, one of the only honest American charities in Uganda. It's not one of the corrupt ones you financially support. What more can you do for me?"

I winced inside and out. Was there any chance that we could maybe *not* berate and shame the U.S. Ambassador to Uganda?

Because, it really would be okay to *not* berate and shame the U.S. Ambassador to Uganda. That really would be perfectly alright with me.

We arrived at the restaurant and the proprietor—another Gloria, which is Gloria #3 for those keeping score at home—informed us that the U.S. Ambassador to Uganda was unfortunately unable to join us. Although I did want to meet him, I was relieved to not have to be caught in the crossfire of a Gran Gloria/Ambassador showdown at the 10 Tables Corral.

I was seated next to Bridget and enjoyed the most lovely meal while talking to her. Early on at dinner, Gloria #2, my tripmate, told Bridget about my wholly unspecific and utterly vague idea of moving to Uganda. Gloria #1, Gran Gloria, yelled out, "He wouldn't last four weeks here!" All of the conversation at the table stopped short. Bridget recovered the fastest, picked up the gauntlet, and took it upon herself to prove Gran Gloria wrong. Bridget detailed how I would adapt, from learning stick shift to where I should look for an apartment. Her explanations were as much for me as they were to show Gran Gloria that I could be successful.

With Bridget's cultivation, that planted seed took root and started to poke out of the ground.

Day 6
November 20, 2012

This was a day to ask questions. I felt it when I woke up this morning. I was determined to ask questions. I was determined to get some answers. I clutched this determination firmly in hand as we arrived on the school grounds.

The changes to the school grounds over the past two years are nothing short of remarkable. In the short time since I was last here in 2010, Gloria's fundraising has dramatically changed the Busingye campus. The school has added a chicken coop with four hundred chickens, providing both protein to the children as well as some income from the sale of the eggs. A sewing studio was built providing both practical skills for the children as well as some income from the sale of the garments. And a modern medical clinic was built and is set to open in a few months, providing both advanced care to the community and some income from the provision of services.

One aspect of the school that has remained unchanged is the hand-lettered signs posted on sturdy trees all around the school grounds. The signs are a mesmerizing mix of elementary school reminders alongside messages that you would first assume were meant for distinctly more adult audiences. A sign reading "Listen to your teacher's advice" is next to "Say no to sex," which is next to "Protect yourself from AIDS and HIV," which is next to "Make friends but never enemies," which is next to "Do not exchange sex for gifts." We're talking nursery school through seventh grade here, folks.

Once we arrived at the school this morning, the group was told that we would be heading out to tour the local community, a trip you will recall that did nothing for me in 2010. So I decided to hang back to finish stuffing the remaining few hundred gift bags with Nurse Liana.

Once the group had left, Gran Gloria launched into a tirade about the soon-to-be-completed clinic, questioning how finances were being handled, and how some staff don't understand that Gloria could withdraw her support *at any damn minute* she chooses. She loves her work, she continued, but she will not (Will. Not.) be disrespected. I had no response. I didn't want to validate this drama but I also really didn't want conflict. I thought it was significant that she waited until our group left before sharing this tirade for my ears only, but I really had no idea what was fueling her approach.

Once we were finished stuffing the bags, I started to wander aimlessly around campus. I quickly ran into Joseph, the headmaster. Right there in front of me was my first opportunity to cross a question off of my list. I was tempted to ask him about the finances about which Gloria had just been complaining a few minutes earlier, but I opted instead for a more self-centered line of questioning.

"Why *Mutebi*?" I asked.

He immediately put his arms in front of him, flexed, and growled, "*Mutebi*!" Ok, not that again.

"Yes. Yes. I know. But what can you tell me about the word?"

"*Mutebi* is a very important clan," Joseph replied and started to walk away. I felt like we were getting somewhere here so I was not prepared to let him go.

"But what are the *Mutebi* like?" I persisted.

"They are cultural leaders," Joseph answered.

Alrighty, now we're talking!

"They keep people together and are destined to be kings. One *Mutebi* is king now," Joseph concluded.

"So you saw those qualities in me and that's why you named me *Mutebi*?" I said trying to put a neat, sparkly bow on this.

"Okay," he replied and started to walk away.

"No," I nudged. "I mean, you see *Mutebi* in me? King-like qualities?"

"Okay," he replied and again started to walk away.

"I bring people together and am destined to be king?" I persevered, not a small amount desperately.

"Okay," he replied and, this time, he really did walk away.

So, there you had it! A firm, assertive, irrefutable declaration of my royal status. Roar. Glub. Glub. Roar!

I was still a little bit embarrassed at yesterday's teaching performance, so I walked into a sixth-grade class that had a period off. After I dispensed with their "You are welcome here, Our Dear American Visitor!" chant, I asked them to teach me more words in Lugandan. By the end of our conversation, I could do a passable version of "Head, Shoulders, Knees, and Toes" that made them all laugh even as I got more than a few thumbs up.

We then gathered around a very-much-no-longer-accurate-map-with-two-Germanies, pointed to different countries and discussed variations in languages, capitals, and climates. Then we talked about their future plans and their thoughts on Uganda. This time, I most certainly did not freeze as I did yesterday. I made them answer in complete sentences, made them give each other flowers, and generally made them participate dutifully.

Now glowing, I left the class and ran right into Assistant Headmaster Linda. I foolishly boasted of my *Musamesa* prowess. "Let us see," she said.

She put her arm through my arm and physically led me back into the classroom. She asked them what they had learned.

Silence.

Linda asked them whether they had been to the map and several students started answering out loud, talking over one another. She chided them for this fundamental breach in classroom etiquette that they hadn't breached with me earlier. "Raise your hands," she admonished and I whispered, "I told them that!" My face was getting pretty red. She asked them what countries they had looked at.

Silence.

Linda led me out of the room and said, "Needs work, *Musamesa* Ken. Needs work." I walked away mumbling about a *musamesa* tree of knowledge that had successfully fallen in the woods that she hadn't been around to hear.

Without question, the highlight of my day was a forty-five-minute dialogue with Tommy, our amazing driver, about the whole "Kill the Gays" legislation. It had now taken me over two years to build up the courage to broach this topic and, even with that amount of time behind me, I was still a bit nervous. I didn't want someone to turn this gay Jew into the local authorities. Tommy actually did his best to put me at ease during what turned out to be a riveting conversation.

As an entry point, I remarked that we don't hear much about Uganda in American media except for one, well-publicized piece of legislation.

"The gay one?" Tommy asked.

"Yes," I replied.

He began by remarking that the government was being too harsh and that execution was severe. I knew Tommy was exponentially more liberal than his Ugandan peers, owing to his extensive knowledge of American culture and his white, Jewish Canadian wife (she whose brother says "Good on ya!"). Nevertheless, this was still a relief of a good start.

"I know some gay people," Tommy remarked. "There are women with whom I play rugby who are gay." I want an award for suppressing a snarky reply about lesbians and sports which likely wouldn't have resonated comedy-wise with Tommy anyway.

Tommy then went on to question what it is that "these gays even want." He explained that Ugandans are intensely private people. They do not kiss in public, be they straight or gay. He kept returning to the refrain, "Gays should just do their own thing as long as they keep it private."

This was a bit of a different take than the ubiquitous American cliché of anti-gay pundits asserting that they have no problem with gays as long they don't flaunt it. Here in Uganda, no one flaunts anything private: gay or straight. So Tommy again asked, "What do the gays want?"

"To not be killed or jailed?" I threw out there.

"And they shouldn't be," Tommy responded.

The heartbreaking piece of the conversation was when Tommy explained that previously it was happenstance, common, and in some places, even *expected* for two men close in friendship, familial, or clan-based bond to hold hands or embrace. Now, those physical interactions are being second-guessed, cast in a new, nefarious light.

"You see it less and less but it used to be like this," Tommy said as he stood before me and grabbed both of my forearms. He gripped and stroked my arms as he looked in my eyes. "This is how brothers by blood or friendship talked."

When he was physically touching me, my heart rate quickened, and I immediately felt embarrassed. My gut reaction was the thought that something romantic lay at the core of his touch. I wasn't sure whether my interpretation was my American lens or my gay glasses or a combination of the two. I looked at his hand on my forearms and tried to recast the physical touch as something more about human connection than romantic touch.

As I caught a glimpse of something plaintive in Tommy's eyes, I grasped a small piece of understanding. My embarrassment quickly turned to grief, mourning the loss of any piece of Ugandan culture where the fire of connection was snuffed out by fear. It was quite a lot to take in and I was only scratching the surface for two seconds. I could barely wrap my mind around the loss felt by those whose culture was actually being suppressed here. This wasn't just about gay people in Uganda; this was about an entire culture being shaped by some American churches in the Midwest who were pouring money and resources into more susceptible locales where their fear would take root.

Even worse, that petty assault was unquestionably and tragically working.

Day 7
November 21, 2012

Gloria #2, Gloria the Younger, wanted to put a checkmark next to her bucket list item of "Went for a run in Uganda." Although it wasn't necessarily on my list, I agreed to go with her as I anticipated that it would be a memorable experience. So, there we were this morning, going for a jog at 6:30 a.m. along the streets of Masaka. Ugandans don't generally go for runs, so we were certainly a site to see: two crazy *mazungas* (white people) decked out in our Under Armour ceremonial dress, bounding gazelle-like over potholes. We didn't get very far as the streets and sidewalks were not set up for casual runners, but it was still fun to get out there and hit the pavement engaged in a physical activity that was the utmost in head-clearing.

Back at the school, our schedule either fell apart or there really wasn't much for us to do. I wasn't really sure which was correct, as there weren't tasks for us to complete, but there was still a sense given to us by Gran Gloria that she had plans for us that didn't pan out. Other than stuffing those bags and whatever we were going to be asked to do at the Christmas party tomorrow, we "Dear American Visitors" may have been welcome at Busingye, but we didn't have a ton of purpose. Consequently, we were left with close to three hours of free time today.

As I was again wandering aimlessly across the grounds, Assistant Headmaster Linda yelled out, "*Musamesa* Ken, your social studies class with the P6 (sixth graders) is at 11:15 a.m." I was never really sure if Linda was joking, so I erred on the side of taking her at her word. I told her that I was not prepared and that I needed to read the book. She called my bluff and took me by the arm to the library to tour the books. Although it turned out that she was *mostly* joking about the 11:15 a.m. class, she was pressing me pretty hard about my course plans when (*when*, not *if*, mind you) I return in May.

We talked for a spell about academics and then I took a chance and put one foot in the "Gays in Uganda Conversational Thunderdome." I had a strong sense that Linda would tow more of a hardline than Tommy. Throughout the week, she has referenced God in conversations that I thought were decidedly more secular, and her arms were pretty constantly outstretched to the heavens above in church on Sunday. I figured I would receive more of a conservative outlook from Assistant Headmaster Linda. And oh how I was right.

I successfully used the same entry point via American media coverage of Uganda that I used with Tommy yesterday. Although Linda started by denouncing the killing of people, she hoped there would be another way to have those gay people come back to their senses, another way to discipline them. She insisted that gay people must understand that Adam was lonely and that God created Eve to be his companion. There had to be a way, she fervently urged, of educating the gay people to return to the only acceptable biblical understanding of a man being with a woman.

She then concluded, almost in an offhand sort of way, that there was a financial aspect to all of this.

"How so?" I asked.

Linda explained that when the media is involved, there is money present somewhere. She declared that there is some financial gain for gay people in pushing forward their presence, although she was not entirely able to pinpoint where that gain took place. "Someone is getting rich somewhere," she concluded. "That is how it always works here."

This was a much different conversation than my conversation with Tommy, mostly due to the fact that it wasn't a conversation. I really had nothing to offer. My part was to listen and be respectful which I did and I was. My fear level had certainly increased during this dialogue. I had no interest in telling Linda that I was gay, as I didn't want to alter our relationship. Her views were so rooted in faith and I assumed that there wasn't much a gay Jewish American could do to influence a Pentecostal Ugandan. Not that I was necessarily trying to influence her, even as I had many snarky replies regarding Eve and that snake.

I bid Linda adieu and walked by a group of girls washing dishes. Flashing back to my experience washing dishes with the girls two years ago, my excitement immediately rocketed up to epic proportions, and *let me tell you!* These girls did not disappoint. We talked about boys and the girls laughed that boys are still super lazy. We talked about their futures and they revealed their aspirations to be doctors and nurses with one lawyer thrown into the mix. This was a far cry from the unanimously expressed vocation of teaching that the girls expressed to me when I was first in Uganda. And we talked about their plans to leave Uganda, a deep desire that each one of them affirmed. Further—and this was huge—they told me that *Mutebi* were kind, humble, and polite. So there you had it! An assertive, irrefutable declaration of my character.

Toward the end of the day, I sat with *Musawu* Nurse Liana and I decided to have another go at the Gays in Uganda thread. I would like to pause here and note I wasn't as close to Liana as I had been during my first trip to Uganda. Going into this trip, I had questions about the way she approached her position as the school nurse, as there had been so much drama regarding those medical records a few years ago. But I ultimately decided that it truly was not my business. So I left it alone.

We have been super cordial all week, but the vibe she was giving off was vaguely flirty. Her confidence seemed much increased since we first met, but she was making me a little bit uncomfortable. I didn't want to cultivate more relationship-building conversations than were absolutely necessary.

I eschewed the pretense of talking about the American media coverage of Uganda and just asked her how she thought gay people should be treated in Uganda. She thought for a minute and replied, "As a nurse, the gays should probably not be killed." The combination of a "as a nurse" and a "probably" right before referencing execution threw me off. I was reasonably sure that the Hippocratic oath wasn't, "People in medicine should *probably* do no harm."

She described homosexuals as abnormal as she laughed and ruminated, "Maybe life in prison would help them." I didn't know what to do with her laugh. It took quite a bit for me to bite back a retort of, "Sure! Maybe! Couldn't hurt anyone to find out, y'know?"

Finally, Nurse Liana added that there was obviously a financial aspect to all of this. That little gem again? But this time, Nurse Liana had more of an explanation than Assistant Headmaster Linda. Liana explained that Europeans come to Uganda and offer people money to be gay and join their group. I was stunned by this information, because I thought it was either (a) horseshit, or (b) true.

And if it were true, then there are some Europeans who are *way* past due on my account. And my interest rates are pretty fucking steep.

Regardless, Liana's response made me wonder what I was even doing asking these questions. I wasn't trying to change anyone's mind and the responses I was receiving seemed to make me feel progressively more uncomfortable. I thanked her and moved on to other topics. She again asked about my wife. I again told her that her hair looked pretty.

The rest of the day was spent giving each of the thousand-plus boys and girls a brand new outfit and their goodie bag. But, they could only get them from Gran Gloria's hand, usually as they curtsied. Again, Gloria was the one who had put this all together, but the distribution method made me cringe. Every child curtsied before her and it felt very, "Kneel before the pharaoh" as I was off to side thinking, *Let my people go!* Only, these weren't my people.

Even so, the children were so genuinely appreciative. Those new outfits were royal finery in the children's eyes and the googly-eye rings were priceless signets. You couldn't help but watch and smile as the children beamed. So I did my best to just watch and smile.

Day 8
November 22, 2012

Somehow, this is our last day at the school. And it was missionary shirt day. Oh how I missed missionary shirt day. The five of us arrived on campus decked out in our beige, short-sleeved Gloria's Children collar shirts. The uniform serves no functional purpose but Gran Gloria said it made for great pictures for her fundraising literature, so there you go.

Our first hour was free, so I caught up with Betty, the daughter of Joseph the headmaster. Betty is twenty years old and teaches history at a college in Masaka. She is currently taking a break from that life and hanging around the school. I was excited to hear how Betty, an emissary from a younger generation, framed the gays in Uganda issue. As Betty's father is not only the head-master but also a reverend, I figured she would have an especially informed and nuanced perspective.

I didn't even finish phrasing the question, "How do you think gays in Uganda should be treated?" before she cut in.

"The gays should be executed," she said.

"Go on," I prodded, waiting for either a disclaimer or the hushed whispers of liberal dissent she did not want her father to hear. I inched toward her.

"No, that's it," she replied. "Killing the gays would be a good example to other gay people to no longer choose to be gay."

"Can you say more on that?" I gently asked, slowly moving a little bit closer to give her room to say what she *actually* felt as opposed to the lines clearly fed to her by her father.

"The gays should be killed," Betty said. "Without question."

I immediately backed away from Betty the Bloody.

At 11 a.m. today, November 22nd, it was quite naturally time for the Christmas party. We walked to the central courtyard where all thousand-plus students were assembled. The choir was singing "*Feliz Navidad*," which, contextually, I did not understand, but which melodically I still enjoyed. The children then did their rendition of the nativity complete with a white girl doll with blond pigtails playing the part of Baby Jesus. The image of that specific doll in the hands of these Ugandan children was a sight both hilarious and disturbing.

Gran Gloria cut the cake and handfuls of crumbs were given out to every child. Then the five of us served lunch to all of the children. I doled out a purple (yes purple) peanut sauce to my vegetarian brothers and sisters. I then beelined it over to the girls doing dishes. At this point, dishwashing was the equivalent of my safe place. But good conversation was not to be had this time around. The dishwashing area was moved to the center of campus, in easy view of the teachers. We were constantly admonished to wash faster, as there were only 250 plates for one thousand children. Quick turnover was key. Eventually, my position was effectively terminated via being nudged out of the circle by faster hands. I decided to leave this experience off of my work history so that I would not have to explain my firing to future employers.

I went back to work the food line with the rest of the group. Tommy and I were sliding bowls of meat down the line. He asked whether I had initiated any further conversations about gay people in Uganda. I told him about my disturbing conversation with Betty the Bloody.

"Then you better be careful," he laughed, "or she might try to kill *you.*"

I laughed in return and then the full import of his words hit me. He knew! He knew I was gay! Suddenly, I realized that I was gay and out in Uganda. Even if it was only to one person. It felt amazing! Also, it felt a little bit scary! I really didn't want Betty the Bloody to find out.

After lunch, I somehow ended up sorting boxes with Betty the Bloody and Nurse Liana. Headmaster Joseph walked in. Before I could greet him, Betty the Bloody, his daughter, said, "Father, *Musamesa* Ken wants to know about gays in Africa." This was an extraordinarily uncomfortable moment for me. In the prior conversations with Tommy, Linda, Liana, and Betty, *I* had been the one to initiate the dialogue. Losing control of that was unnerving. Losing control of that in a room with the nurse who thought the gays *probably* should not be killed, Betty the Bloody who thought gays should *definitely* be killed, and Joseph who was the *reverend father* of Betty the Bloody who thought gays should *definitely* be killed? Yeah, that was downright unsettling.

Joseph surprised me though. Sure, he was 100 percent anti-gay and he thought gays should be preached at until they changed. But he didn't think that gay people should be killed. So take that, murderous wayward daughter! Joseph then started talking about Adam and Eve, but having already heard this biblical tale from Assistant Headmaster Linda, I zoned out a bit and continued to sort boxes as he talked.

Next thing I knew, Joseph was physically poking me hard on my chest. Like actually poking me. And I got scared. But then I realized he was at the climax of the story when Eve was created via Adam's rib and he was poking my chest to emphasize that point in the story. He then asked me what I thought should be done with the gay people in Uganda. He was the first person to actually ask for my opinion and I faltered. My options felt like they were (a) espouse a humanitarian view that underscores how each life is precious and no one person should be restricted, or (b) recognize the cultural sensitivity issues at play here and frame a response that respects Ugandan culture even as I slightly challenged the notion that something is to be gained by executing their brothers and sisters.

I then heard myself reply, "Well, your daughter Betty wants to kill people and that doesn't sound very biblical to me," and when he turned toward his demon offspring, I made a hasty exit out of that room. Turns out, I had chosen to go with option (c) deflection and escape.

The rest of the day was spent watching the 147 students in Top Class (kindergarten) graduate to P1 (first grade). Each of the four- and five-year olds donned pint-sized little caps and gowns and it was, of course, the cutest thing you could ever imagine. Many of the parents and guardians attended and each child and their family posed for a picture with Gran Gloria who was also inexplicably decked out in a cap and gown. The remarks at the ceremony were largely about Gran Gloria, with nary a mention of their teachers. The families thanked Gran Gloria profusely when they came up to take their photo with the woman, the myth, the legend.

The children then sang a song, which had three verses repeated seven—oh yes, seven—times. One verse was dedicated solely and exclusively to welcoming Teacher Kenny to the school, and, lest you get confused, let me be perfectly clear: Teacher Kenny is me! They were singing a song about me! It was as close to "Layla" or "Roxanne" as I was ever likely to get, so I soaked it all in. All seven times.

There was more dancing, a few more tributes to Gran Gloria, and then it was time to board the Land Cruiser out of campus one last time. The first time I left in 2010, I knew I would never be back. This time, that absolute certainty was not present. The last person to bid me farewell was Assistant Headmaster Linda and she made a comment about how excited she was for me to return to teach there. In that moment, it almost felt possible.

Day 9
November 23, 2012

Last day. A day of reckoning. A day, hopefully, of reconciliation of all of the conflicting emotions playing bumper cars in my head. For days now, I have been dreading the penning of these last words as I don't really feel ready to work through my thoughts. But I also know that I can't endlessly avoid writing this last entry even as I clearly don't have all of the answers.

So why not delay a little bit more and run through my day? We woke up. Ate a little. Stopped by the Equator again. Shopped some in Kampala. Had a late lunch. Went to the airport. And now I am in Nairobi on a layover before an eight-and-a-half-hour flight to Paris, which is before an eight-and-a-half-hour flight to New York. And sadly, that run-through didn't buy me nearly as much time as I thought it would.

As I sit in this airport and reflect on my two experiences in Uganda, my focus keeps coming back to Gran Gloria. She was the reason I came to Uganda in the first place and she was an integral part of my inspiration for returning. I feel that if I could somehow resolve my issues with Gloria, everything else would become clear. It became my Ugandan *Sound of Music* quandary: how *do* you solve a problem like Gloria?

There are things I have written about Gloria on these pages in the past few days and on those pages two years ago that have made me cringe. Literally cringe. As the ink hit the paper, I would

150

immediately feel like an ass, a traitor, a complete personification of betrayal incarnate. Even now as I write this, Gloria is sitting less than three feet in front of me. I actually just measured the distance with my hands. But as bad as I have felt, I also have been trying so hard to not let her behavior distort my chronicling of our interactions in this journal.

Maybe it would help me frame my Gloria quandary if I focused on the facts.

> **FACT #1**: Since 2003, Gloria Thomas has raised hundreds of thousands of dollars for the Busingye Advanced Primary and Day Care School.
>
> **FACT #2**: With that funding, wells have been dug, stoves have been installed, and new classroom buildings have been constructed.
>
> **FACT #3**: A library was built and the shelves populated with actual books.
>
> **FACT #4**: Blankets, clothes, shoes, and socks have been supplied to thousands and thousands of children.
>
> **FACT #5**: There's a new playground, a building for milling corn, and the previously mentioned chicken coop, sewing building, and medical clinic.
>
> **FACT #6**: During the day, students use new school supplies at new desks.
>
> **FACT #7**: At night, the school now has solar lights for safety and the orphans sleep on new beds.
>
> **FACT #8**: Under Gloria's patronage, the school's student population has increased from 434 to one thousand.
>
> **FACT #9**: 100 percent of the P7 students have taken their P7 exams and graduated. This statistic is unheard of and cannot be found anywhere else in Uganda. Truly.

There were a few times during the trip when I witnessed Gloria's brash and culturally dissonant approach and thought, "Yeah, but I'm sure things would have been fine without Gloria

Thomas." That is a lie, a total falsehood. You cannot scroll through the list of accomplishments detailed above (and I left many out!) and put forth any emotion other than complete admiration and gratitude for what Gloria has accomplished. She has changed and *saved* the lives of thousands and thousands of Ugandans: students, teachers, staff, families, and surrounding villagers.

With that assertion, I desperately want my next line to be "The End." But that doesn't feel right either.

There are other layers to this story. And if it is a story, and this journal is the tale, then I am the protagonist because it's my journal. But if I am the protagonist, that means I have set up Gloria as the antagonist. But Gloria isn't the antagonist. The real antagonists are corrupt governments, corporate greed, and a global populace that isn't doing nearly enough to address poverty. But here I am casting a five-foot-four-and-a-half-inch, plucky, ballsy humanitarian as my foil (and, yes, I actually just paused in the writing of that to ask her for her height). Even if we barely touch the surface of feminist theory, you have to question how much of the crap I have given Gloria has to do with gender. But, I'm not fully prepared to go there.

I have actually been having interactions with Gloria all week, but I have been saving my reflections on them until now. I mean, at one point she flat-out declared that she doesn't even really like children that much. Even now, I'm not sure what it is that I really want out of this woman, that thing I can't articulate but am clearly not getting. I'm not really sure what the point would be of penning the litany of "objectionable comments" I have heard her make.

Gloria #2 just poked me in the arm and asked, "You figure her out yet?"

I replied, "Nope. I haven't entirely figured her out yet. But I think that Gloria . . . " and Gloria #2 interrupted me.

"No, no," she said. "I asked if you've figured *it* out yet. As in, from which end of this waiting room we will be boarding the plane. Not everything is about Gloria, Ken"

And with that clarification, the heavens opened up, the seas of discontent parted, the halogen light bulb flashed on, and all of the other metaphors went all metaphorical.

For the past eight days and for twelve days in 2010, I had been framing my experience through the lens of Gloria. I'm struggling? Well, you wouldn't believe what Gloria just said. I'm feeling overwhelmed? Well, you wouldn't believe how Gloria just treated Nurse Liana. I'm in transition and lacking in purpose? Well, Gloria blah blah negative blah blah insensitive blah blah roar blah glub.

And thus, my friends, we have Ken Schneck's well-traveled and most entertaining three-ring circus. To the left, feast your eyes on the death-defying antics of Escapism. In the center ring, be hypnotized and stupefied by the magic of Deflection. And in that last ring, I dare you to resist that seductive siren of song, Displacement. <pause for applause>

Focusing on Gloria and her antics is just plain easy. It's easy to transfer all of my angst away from me and onto Gloria. In this moment, and hopefully also when I read it aloud, I see this for what it is. And what it is, friends, well that would be jealousy. Jealousy for what Gloria has accomplished. Envy for how she has been adopted by these people. Resentment for the reverence that is heaped onto Gran Gloria.

It is a foolproof strategy to focus on the fact that Gloria is not behaving the way I would behave if I were providing her humanitarian efforts than it is for me to focus on the fact that I am, in no way, providing those humanitarian efforts myself. I'm a backseat driver with no title to the car, no driver's license, and no sense of how we should get to where we want to go. But I've made damn sure to critique the driver by writing about her in my journal in the backseat, never once myself suggesting we take a left at the fork in the road up ahead.

So the real *Sound of Music* question for Uganda Act 2 is: how do we solve a problem like *Musamesa Mutebi* Ken? What can I do to stop deflecting and escaping and displacing? How do I turn the magnifying glass inward to take these incredible opportunities I have had in Uganda and actually *do* something with them?

I can't help but think that being more realistic would help. That simple adjustment to my approach would alter my conclusions and address all of the lies, half-truths, and rationalizations I have penned. No more promising dentist chairs when I never realistically was going to make that call to secure one. No more pretending I'm moving to Uganda in May when I never realistically was entertaining the idea. No more asserting that Gran Gloria is the question to be answered when the real queries realistically were all about me.

But, more than anything, I need to relax. Just plain relax: relax with the meaning-making business, relax with the search for Truth, relax with the idea that everything can be solved with just the right words. Do I keep asking questions? Yes. But maybe I could *not* go nuts trying to figure out the answers? Because that would be okay.

I might not have actually figured out what *Mutebi* means, but I can still tattoo the name on my forearm (which I did). I might not actually discover how the gays can survive in this land, but I can still urge changes to take place so that LGBT people do not have to live in fear and Uganda can retain beautiful human parts of her culture. I might not figure out what drives Gran Gloria, but I can still admire her efforts even as I decry her method of delivery as being the textbook example of cultural dissonance.

And, above all else, I might not fully comprehend the concept of *Tulibaluganda*, that overarching umbrella that we are all brethren. I might not live it. I might not embody it. Heck, I might not even always spell it right. But I can still try to pass on a small piece of it.

From Uganda.

Through me.

To you.

Which I hope I just did.

Rocky Mountains
COLORADO

The Summit of It All

(Colorado Rocky Mountains:
June 14, 2015 – June 21, 2015)

Day 1
June 14, 2015

I started out this entry by writing the words, "How did I get into this strange mess?" Then I paused. Then I smiled. And then I crossed out those words.

I clearly ask that question a lot. And if I ask that question a lot, it means that I find myself in a lot of strange messes. And if I find myself in a lot of strange messes, it might very well mean that this, well, this is just what I do. This is where I find myself. This is who I am. And if that's the case, then maybe I should stop questioning the strangeness of my messes or even that the messes exist in the first place. Instead, I should just dive in, describe the mess, and see whether I can't get started on that making of meaning process straightaway.

This time around I am standing at a whole different altitude, emotionally and physically. Shockingly, the easier piece for me to describe is the emotional side of my life. I think I might actually be in a good headspace. Read that sentence again. Yeah, even my own eyes widen when I reread that sentence, so I can only imagine how much those words would dilate the pupils of those who have read the pages that have come before. But we'll put that shock on pause for a moment and describe the physical changes to my life.

After burning out personally and professionally in Vermont, I cast an extraordinarily wide net to relocate my body, soul, professional energy, and feline companion. And like so many soul-searchers before me who were desperately seeking a fresh start, I landed in that mecca of change, that hub of rejuvenation, that center for catharsis: Cleveland. Yes, Cleveland. In Ohio.

Having never spent a minute of my professional life working outside of higher education, the thought of leaving the employ of colleges and universities was too overwhelming an idea to contemplate. But the idea of staying immersed in administration, knee-deep in alcohol and other drug drama, sexual misconduct miasma, and hyper-involved parent problems? Well, that was also too overwhelming an idea to contemplate. I knew I wanted to move over to the wonderful world of teaching, but my public record of academic achievement consisted of assorted rants in *The Huffington Post*, years of gabbing on my own gay radio show, and the occasional speaking gig to obscure audiences who understood the L's and the G's, but thought the B's were a phase and were completely miffed by those pesky T's. None of this work amounted to a solid academic pedigree.

Amazingly, I stumbled across an institution of higher education that valued teaching far more than publishing, and I was able to secure a tenure-track position as a professor delivering content on how to navigate the drama, miasma, and problems on college campuses. Now that I was no longer working as an administrator, I suddenly wasn't taking work home with me. I suddenly wasn't holding a pager as I had been for the past sixteen years (and, yes, institutions located in areas where cell phone coverage is spotty still use pagers). I suddenly could have one of those mythical social lives about which I had often heard but had certainly never experienced. It was a whole new world of possibilities.

The only drawback: Cleveland. Which apparently was in some state called Ohio. Which apparently was in some part of the country called the Midwest. I had always thought the Midwest was a snarky metaphor. Turns out, no, it's an actual place. Other than that rained out trip to Disneyland, AIDS/LifeCycle, Esalen, and assorted airport layovers, I had never stepped foot west of the Northeast for more than a few days at a time. But oddly, it didn't faze me to move to parts unknown in states with more vowels than consonants, a quality that used to make me instantly distrust a destination.

I don't think there was any way I could have moved from New York City to Cleveland. But Vermont to Cleveland didn't seem that bad. In fact, resources- and social-life-wise, the move represented an upgrade from Vermont. Plus, I didn't tell people about the move too far in advance nor, true to Ken form, did I do any research on my own. So, I didn't even know that Cleveland had a reputation for anything other than "locale not in Vermont that had a job for me," which represented the totality of my criteria.

Simple as that, I boxed up my apartment, left Vermont, and moved to Cleveland. My new employer arranged for a moving company to load up those boxes and transport them out west. All I needed to do was pack up my car with some clothes, some books, and Jack Rocket Cat, and get them all to Cleveland. I was actually nervous about this last item as Jack can be a nightmare when it comes to new things, much like his human caretaker/food-giver. Previous attempts to get him into his carrier for annual vet visits were scratch-filled tantrums with loud, feline cries of protest throughout the entire eight-minute drive to his vet. The drive to Cleveland was going to be eight *hours*, which I deduced to be more than eight minutes. I was dreading Jack's reaction.

On the morning of our departure to Cleveland, I put out Jack's carrier, opened the door, and sighed as I steeled myself for the fisticuffs. I walked over to where I thought he was hiding under the couch, heard a rustle behind me, turned around, and there was Jack: snuggled in his carrier, purring. He looked at me and I heard him say, "Seriously, we *must* get out of Vermont. Let's. Freakin'. Go!" I think he would have closed the carrier door behind him if he were physically able. Damn you, Evolution and that feline lack of opposable thumbs! He meowed once when we crossed the border eight-plus hours later into Cleveland, but, otherwise, he was silent the entire ride. It was an amazing portent of good things to come.

A significantly less amazing portent of good things to come was my moving van that seemed to have taken a slight detour. The original plan, as outlined by the moving company, was:

1. Pack up Ken's belongings.
2. Leave Vermont.
3. Travel to Ohio.
4. Deliver Ken's belongings.

SERIOUSLY...WHAT AM I DOING HERE?

The *actual* plan that the moving company executed was:
1. Pack up Ken's belongings.
2. Leave Vermont.
3. Park the truck in a warehouse in Massachusetts.
4. Wait fifteen days.
5. Travel to Ohio.
6. Deliver Ken's belongings.

Having never utilized a moving company before, I suddenly had both a new appreciation for words like *estimated* and *window of time* as well as a significantly greater acceptance for those pesky *things about which I couldn't do a damn thing to change.*

When the answer to the question, "Can you tell me exactly where the truck is right now?" is "I'm not sure what you mean, sir," well, that's a special kind of feeling. There truly was nothing I could do to change my situation, and my situation was me, sitting in an empty two-bedroom apartment in Cleveland, Ohio with a cat, my computer, and a few items of clothing.

Though it is *possible* that I complained about the lack of my stuff to my friends and family a few hundred times each hour, this scenario was the best thing that could have happened to me. After quickly going through two new air mattresses and realizing that buying Jack some toys would prevent me from having to go through buying any more new air mattresses, having my belongings nowhere near me forced me to get out into the world. Don't get me wrong: I was a banshee on the phone with the moving company every four or five hours, but in the interim, I was out exploring Cleveland. I said "Yes" to every invite, accepted every offer to connect, and aggressively pursued every offhand remark of "We should get together sometime." On my first night, I joined a gay tennis group. On my first full day, I discovered an oasis of a park right in my backyard with views overlooking the ocean (locals keep calling it a "lake," but it sure looks like an ocean to me). And at every other waking minute, I explored Cleveland's truly incredible food scene.

Things only got better once my belongings arrived. I loved my apartment. I started work and adored being solely in the classroom. I felt like I was making actual friends who knew nothing of my life in Vermont and really didn't care about it all that much. I even returned to the stage doing stand-up comedy under the guise of "storytelling events" and "hosting burlesque shows." One year after moving to Cleveland, I bought a house and acquired a housemate who is both an amazingly inspiring woman and one of the top pastry chefs in the city. All this is to say, I have concluded that I really like this Cleveland-Midwestern thing!

Now, this is not to say that there weren't significant missteps in my past two years here. My first year as a full-time professor was far from smooth sailing, as my structure-light, student-led style of content delivery that worked so well in Vermont instead fell so unbelievably flat in Ohio. There was that one day that a particularly vocal student critic of mine remarked out loud, in class, "I mean, fine, I guess we'll do it your way instead of a way that has actual value." That was not a highlight for me.

My first year of dating was far from smooth sailing as my frenetic, stream-of-consciousness style that worked so well in my social circle in Vermont instead fell so flat with the men of Cleveland. There was that one day that I agreed to let the man I had been dating move in with me. I picked him up at the airport after he had taken a quick trip home to Seattle to see some friends. When he climbed in the car, I gave him a rose and a key to my house with a ribbon on it. He gave me a bag of airplane pretzels and remarked out loud, in the airport parking lot, that instead of moving in with me that day, he would be moving back to Seattle to be with his ex. That was not a highlight for me.

My first year of trying to distance myself from the activity and emotions of Vermont was far from smooth sailing, as my daily recounts of small-town Vermont politics and interpersonal small-town drama that worked so well with the Vermont liberals fell so flat in Ohio. There was that one day when my still-daily online reading of the local Vermont newspaper was interrupted by an email from my ex-husband in Vermont letting me know that he had put our dog down. It wasn't out loud. It wasn't on the phone. It was through an email and I was devastated on so many levels. That was not a highlight for me.

But there have been so many more victories than defeats here in Cleveland, and this third summer here presented one of the most alien opportunities for victory that I have ever experienced: three months off. My first summer in Cleveland was spent waiting for my belongings to arrive and setting up my life. My second summer here was spent moving into my new house, settling up my life, and trying to laugh off the departure of the Seattle guy. My third summer here—this summer—was a blank slate. I have never done particularly well with blank slates; one could argue that I get into trouble when there is no structure present around me. So, the goal was to find some sort of huge activity that would occupy a few weeks of my time and would challenge me in heretofore new ways.

So here I sit, in a hotel in Denver, Colorado, on the night before I'm embarking on an eight-day backpacking journey in the Colorado Rocky Mountains. The "how I got here" is as impulsive as it has ever been. Somehow, I do oddly feel some consistency in my modus operandi, which each time looks something like this:

Thought → Website → Register

I just do things like this sometimes. I act. I chase impulses. Rinse and repeat. I make last-minute purchases at the register. I get a tattoo that hadn't occurred to me the day before. I get married. I go to Uganda. I pedal hundreds of miles. I go to hippie retreats for healing. I act. I chase impulses.

This experience already feels different than the ones that have come before. This trip is so far out of my comfort zone, it is truly laughable. Let's consider the path ahead:

1. Here in Colorado, I will be sleeping for seven nights out in the wilderness when the closest I have ever come to this

was sleeping in the back of a truck for a few nights in a mobile city on a catered AIDS ride.

2. Here in Colorado, I will hike with a backpack on my shoulders when the closest I have ever come to this was hiking a few hours through the flat land of the Cuyahoga Valley National Park, never more than a mile from a vending machine in the dire worst-case scenario that the thirst got real.

3. Here in Colorado, I will rock climb and repel, when the closest I have ever come to these activities was to use the words as metaphors.

4. Here in Colorado, I will execute a solo overnight when the closest I have ever come to this was weathering a solitary evening without electricity in my house with a dead cell phone.

5. Have I ever gone camping? Never.

6. Have I ever lived with no bathroom facilities? Nope.

7. Have I ever experienced flora and fauna? Do documentaries count? No? Then no.

But when I act, when I follow impulse, I go all in. And for me, that meant signing up with Outward Bound, an organization that has a solid reputation for changing lives, providing introspection, and messing with your head. I have been assured that the last one happens only in the healthiest of ways.

I'm blessedly not completely overwhelmed with paralyzing anxiety when I think about the eight days ahead because I simply don't know that much about the eight days ahead. The staff of Outward Bound hasn't told me much. Like, at all. The itinerary I was emailed a few days ago contained maybe fourteen or fifteen words, none of them descriptive. So, to fill in the blanks, my mind has become grounded in the following Manifesto of Ken Schneck's Expectations:

Expectation #1 – I can handle the physicality of this trip. It's just walking. I know how to walk. And how heavy could that backpack really be? Eight pounds? Nine pounds? I'm sure I'll be fine.

Expectation #2 – Eight days away from social media—the longest I have probably gone since Prodigy crashed on our Apple IIe (look it up, kids)—will be a freeing experience.

Expectation #3 – It's not going to rain.

Expectation #4 – I will not get a single blister. Not one single blister the entirety of the trip no matter how new these boots are. Not one blister even in the unlikely scenario in which I just bought these boots a few days ago and didn't take the time to break them in. Which, y'know, is kinda what happened.

Expectation #5 – Pooping in the woods will be a piece of cake.

Expectation #6 – There will be cake.

Expectation #7 – I'm going to get something out of this, a breakthrough I didn't know I needed, an insight I didn't anticipate, a revelation of epic proportions that will stay with me for all the days to come.

I just do things like this. I act. I chase impulse. Am I slightly freaking out right now? Sure. How could I not be? But I am also curious. And that curiosity is moving me forward. Forward toward what? I have no flipping clue. But I will soon find out.

Day 2
June 15, 2015

I think people who know me might not be able to recognize me when I begin experiences such as these. I am not always the chatterbox who can fill up silences. Sometimes when I get overwhelmed, I clam up. Sometimes when I am around new people, I clam up. Sometimes when I feel far from home and any remote sense of comfort, I clam up. We're talking about total and complete tight-lipped silence here. Sure, I can sport a somewhat convincing fake smile on my face, but that fakery of a smile in no way permeates my being. Sometimes, I just can't get out of my own way and today was a master class in just that.

I woke up at 5:30 a.m., well before the 6:30 a.m. alarm I had set for myself. When I went to bed last night, there was no question that a fitful night's sleep was ahead of me, and the reality of that coming to pass was as unsurprising as it was frustrating. I agonized—like really and truly agonized—over what I was going to wear today. I knew we would be in a van driving four-and-a-half hours to our base camp, so I opted for casual wear, dressing for the outcome of "I'm going to sit in a van!" as opposed to "I'm going to go hike the Colorado Rocky Mountains!" Jeans, tennis socks, sneakers, and a cotton t-shirt were thrown on and then I sat at the edge of the bed waiting for the 7:30 a.m. meeting time to finally arrive.

After sitting on my hands for well over an hour (it did not even occur to me to turn on the television or open a book), I dragged my enormous suitcase behind me to the lobby to try to locate my other tripmates with whom I would be sharing this backpacking experience. They were super easy to find, as the lobby was completely empty save for a group of people who resembled serious-looking hikers with serious-looking hiking clothes and serious-looking hiking backpacks. They were introducing themselves, but I wasn't listening. I couldn't listen. I was too busy staring at the serious-looking hiking clothes and the serious-looking backpacks that the serious-looking hikers were sporting. Fuck me—they were dressed to hike and I was dressed to Netflix!

I blurted out something like, "Ken . . . Cleveland . . . be right back!" I then hurriedly grabbed my suitcase and beelined it straight to the hotel lobby bathroom. They must have thought I was freaked out and wasn't coming back. In related news, I was indeed freaking out and was indeed debating not coming back. But I tried instead to focus solely on the task at hand, which in that moment, was blending in fashion-wise with everyone else.

I was suddenly a ball of sweaty, nervous energy as I threw on hiking-adjacent wardrobe. The jeans were replaced by synthetic pants, the cotton shirt became a synthetic top, the tennis socks were thrown aside in favor of a thicker cotton sock, and the sneakers were buried in my suitcase as I laced up my hardcore new hiking boots, which I was urged to break in before this trip but figured I'd be fine because I'm a tennis player (more on that faulty logic later in the week, I'm sure).

For some reason, all I could think about was a scene in *The Secret of My Success*, a 1987 vehicle for Michael J. Fox in which he is impersonating a business executive even though he technically works in the mailroom. At one point, he needs to quickly execute an executive-to-mailroom wardrobe change and needs to do so as fast as possible so as not to get caught in this double-life-web-of-lies. Of course, a secretary walks in on him in the middle of his wardrobe transition. As I was attempting to execute a manic-urbanite-to-serious-hiker wardrobe change, all I kept thinking was, "Please don't let that secretary walk in. Please don't let that secretary walk in. Please don't let that secretary walk in." Mind you, my prayers weren't just a general plea for no one to walk in; I was truly fixated on that one specific secretary from that one specific 1980s movie walking in on me in that one specific hotel lobby bathroom in Denver, Colorado. My head is a fun place to live in, right?

Somewhat more resembling a hiker—albeit a sweaty hiker—I dashed back to the lobby and basically pretended like I had been wearing my new wardrobe the entire time. There was no way to tell if they noticed and, if they did, cared. But I decided they had already judged me and clearly I had failed. Michael J. Fox didn't get outed until the end of the movie and here I was being exposed as a fraud during the opening credits. Heck, it wasn't even the opening credits yet; we were still watching the trailers for upcoming outdoorsy films.

The four-and-a-half-hour van ride actually went by pretty quickly, which was a testament to the conversations taking place along the way. The target demographic for the trip were teachers who all wanted to add outdoor experiential education to their work. The other six people in the van were either K–12 teachers, had been a K–12 teacher, or someday wanted to be a K–12 teacher when they grew up. As a college professor, I definitely felt like a bit of an outlier, but also a slight bit like an exotic unicorn with my different line of work.

After sitting in my normal state of clammed up silence for the first hour, someone asked me something directly and I willed myself to flip a switch and dive into the conversation. We touched on every topic from teaching techniques to the ESPN documentary about the day of O.J. Simpson's Ford Bronco chase to the crazy news that had just blanketed social media of some NAACP President in Spokane, Washington who said she was black but apparently was not black. It really felt like a great group of seven and there was an instant bond. I remember specifically thinking, "Ok, these six folks are going to be my support this week and I'm going to support them." My default mode is always to think of the world in terms of comic books and this was a group of X-Men with whom I could really team up. I was excited to discover their individual superpowers.

When our van arrived at our base camp, I immediately noticed how many Outward Bound staff there were waiting for our van. Was this a welcome party? Or was this trip going to be so challenging that we truly needed that many staff to keep us from actually dying? I settled on the first option while still leaving room for the second option.

But no, I quickly learned! They weren't staff at all! Turns out, there was another group of participants who lived close to base camp and had arrived here on their own. I instantly decided that we were the Jets and this new group was the Sharks. There was no doubt that there was going to be a rumble at the gym. Or, at least, a rumble at the base camp where our van pulled up.

But no, I quickly learned! This wasn't base camp at all! Base camp was at the top of an insanely steep hill staring down at us from a mile-and-a-half up in the clouds. Ok, but when we got up there, there was most certainly going to be a rumble with this new group of non-van interlopers!

But no, I quickly learned! They weren't interlopers at all! This new group was actually a cool group of ladies. As we hiked up the hill as a group, we had to repeatedly pair off with different folks and share details about our lives. It was then that I learned that—get this!—the Colorado Rocky Mountains are at a whole different altitude than Cleveland, Ohio. And not only a whole different altitude, but a higher one, where breathing feels different. And not just different, but harder. I definitely was struggling to adjust my breathing during those conversations, but as I was already the guy who failed at wardrobe, I refused to be the guy who failed at acclimating to altitude. So I interspersed my detail-sharing with dramatic pauses. There was no way to tell if my conversation partners noticed and, if they did, cared. But I decided they had already judged me and clearly I had failed.

Of note was one partner exchange, with one of the Sharks no less. I made a stupid joke about how happy I was she was offering to be my Sherpa, an offer she never made nor implied. She responded that she would indeed make a "solid llama." I let her know that I would henceforth be referring to her as "Llama" both because of this exchange and because I couldn't remember her name. It was a symbol of our bond and one less name for me to learn, so everyone wins. Llama then let me know that it is common for people to get trail names on these trips and she was excited to come up with mine (as you weren't allowed to name yourself). Out loud, I let her know that it would be perfectly okay if I didn't get a trail name. Inside my head, I never wanted anything more than a trail name ever in my entire life.

Once at base camp, our instructors—who I already loved and trusted—showed us a long tarp tent-like thing, split us into two groups and told us to construct our own using tarps, ropes, and stakes. In thinking about the creation of the Manifesto of Ken Schneck's Expectations, it had not even occurred to me to reflect on tent building. I envisioned that the tents would look like . . . well . . . tents. I did not picture tents looking like a large piece of sturdy fabric that you could somehow MacGyver into a tent with a few stakes, some rope, and a bucket full of gumption. And yet, here we were being asked to do just that.

If people could be split into two categories of "more useful" and "less useful," both groups would remark how I successfully created a new group of "useless." I stared. I felt overwhelmed. I froze. It's possible that I told everyone what a great job they were doing, but I think I may be altering my own memory to add encouragement I neither felt nor provided. Again: I stared. I felt overwhelmed. I froze.

After five-sixths of my group had successfully constructed our tarp tent-like thing, it was time to go through our backpacks and separate items. It was the goal of the Outward Bound instructors to lighten our load of any and all extraneous items. There was a ton of explanation. There were various words of caution. There were even some details on the days ahead including bits about rock climbing, repelling, sleeping in snow, and when to blow the whistle that was now around my neck. I, unfortunately, heard next to none of any of it. I was too busy staring, feeling overwhelmed, and standing frozen in place.

We actually will be here at the base camp for the next two days and we were given the option of either camping outside under the tarps, setting up our gear on the covered porch of our dining lodge, or sleeping inside the lodge. I chose the porch because it was outside, which made me feel like less of a poser, but also, hello, covered!

Llama set her stuff right next to mine.

That unfroze me a bit.

Day 3
June 16, 2015

This was a day of confessions. Tons of them.

    Confession #1 – I slept inside the dining lodge last night. As the bedtime hour got closer and closer, I understood less and less why I shouldn't pass up the opportunity to sleep inside when that opportunity would not be available to me for the vast majority of this Colorado trip. And as my understanding lessened and lessened, I inched closer and closer to the door that led to the inside habitat perfectly made for sleeping.

Confession #2 – Confession #1 is a lie. I did *not* inch closer and closer to the door that led to the inside habitat perfectly made for sleeping. At one point Llama said, "You know there's no shame in sleeping inside, right?" and before she finished saying, "right?," I had gathered my belongings and moved inside lightning fast.

Confession #3 – I'll be sleeping inside tonight too.

Confession #4 – I was really proud of myself at one point today. After a crazy, rainy morning, our group finally set out for some skill-based activities. The first was called a Tyrolean Traverse (a name that had to be told to me at least eleven times before it stuck). Apparently there are many different ways to complete a Tyrolean Traverse; ours consisted of hanging upside down and crossing rain-swollen rapids hand-over-hand on a shaky rope. So, to recap: I've never been camping before but I'm being asked to hang upside-down and cross rain-swollen rapids hand-over-hand on a shaky rope? Sure, that makes a lot of sense.

I needed to see it done first before I could wrap my mind around how this would actually come to pass. Thankfully one of our instructors executed the crossing first for all the group to see. Watching her do it just made sense in my head: you're harnessed to the rope and you're essentially pulling yourself to the other side, facing up (very much *not* facing the rain-swollen rapids), solely using your arm strength.

Suddenly, I flipped a switch and thought, *I can do this!* And, not only did I think, *I can do this!* but I thought, *I can do this first!*

Then I heard someone say, "I'll go first!" and much to the surprise of both the group and the guy writing this, that someone volunteering to go first was me!

I should note that the group was surprised because I had come out of the closet this morning during breakfast as someone who had never before been camping. We were having a group conversation about everyone's skill set. I was reluctant to share how few/zero times I had been either camping or just outside in an unstructured manner, but I was excited to find out who else shared my lack of experience. So I blurted out that I had never been camping and waited to see who would yell back, "Me neither!" Yeah, that would be no one. Even the crickets stopped chirping. This was a group of campers and adventurers. And yet there I was, volunteering to go first across the ravine.

I clipped into the harness, walked right off the ledge, and motored to the other side. It really happened as quickly as it took me to pen those words. The ropes burned my hands a bit and the last ten seconds of the traverse were a bear because they were uphill, but I conquered the challenge quickly, without hesitation, and with no small amount of pride. That was unlike anything I had ever done before and now I could say that I did it, blurred as it was in my mind.

The only unforeseen complication was that after I completed my first-ever Tyrolean Traverse, I was suddenly on the other side of the river all by myself. It was lonely! I watched our group cross one-by-one and did my part to be encouraging and cheer them along. Llama stopped midway through her traverse and I thought, *Oh no! Does she need help? My Llama needs me!* But she was merely pausing to stretch out her arms in exultation, take in the world, and marvel at the surroundings, which included looking *down* at the rain-swollen rapids. She was in the middle of the ravine. Looking down. I looked at her and thought, *Fuck. That.*

It took well over an hour to reunite our entire group on the other side of the river and there was a real feeling of group bonding. Yesterday we didn't really know each other. Today we crossed a river together. And it wasn't even a metaphor! I carried that feeling of pride with me as we set off toward the next skill.

Confession #5 – Hiking is actually a little bit hard. After the Tyrolean Traverse, we had to climb a pretty steep trail. Before the trip, I wasn't super worried about the part of the trip where we would be walking. In my life outside of Colorado, I walk a lot.

Daily, even. But walking with that very heavy backpack up steep terrain? Well, heck, that's a whole different type of walking. And these were only ten-pound daypacks; apparently they are going to get far heavier when we set out tomorrow for the backcountry. How on earth am I going to manage this?

With my confidence plummeting a bit as I struggled to catch my breath, I volunteered to be the caboose, that exalted place at the back of the pack. The woman two people in front of me stopped every thirty feet or so to, in her words, "greet an old friend." These "old friends" were flowers that she had not seen in years. I tried to honor her sentiment. I tried to respect her transcendent headspace. I tried to celebrate her very explicitly expressed feelings of joy. I tried for three or four seconds, but then I got annoyed as all of the stopping and starting was making the hike so much more strenuous. But then I felt really bad that I was so annoyed (and holy hell was I annoyed!). She had a fervent fervor for flora and I wish I had been more supportive than annoyed (and holy hell was I annoyed!).

Confession #6 – I fell apart today. I didn't see it coming. And it has really thrown me off. Look, I knew this experience would be hard, but I didn't anticipate completely falling apart. Not on Day 2. And, yet, even so, I fell apart today. On Day 2.

The second skill-based activity we would be executing today was repelling off of a cliff. Like, an actual cliff. And not just repelling off a cliff to the ground, but repelling off of a cliff to the top of another cliff. This last detail was a salient piece of information as our starting point was incredibly high up. I'm not an individual blessed with the skill to estimate distance. For me, there is ground level, high up, and incredibly high up. Using these metrics, I determined our starting point to be incredibly high up.

Although I was certainly nervous, I figured I could power through the repelling activity as I did the Tyrolean Traverse. The problem here was that, instead of going first, I would be the eleventh to repel off the cliff. As tripmate after tripmate disappeared over the edge, my anxiety grew and grew. Suddenly "incredibly high up" started feeling like an inadequate label for our altitude and I invented a new category of "impossibly high up." This new category certainly did nothing to lessen my anxiety.

Continuing my theme of 1980s movies suddenly dominating my thought patterns, I immediately flashed to that part of the movie *Big* where the twelve-year old in the body of adult Tom Hanks finds himself in an executive meeting, listening to a pitch for a new toy. It was a robot that transformed into a skyscraper. The twelve-year old just keeps repeating, "I don't get it." over and over again. That was me. I just didn't understand how this repelling thing worked; I could not wrap my mind around the mechanics. I stepped gingerly toward the edge of the cliff to watch the process, but there was also the part where this meant that I was inching closer to the edge of a cliff and that was something that I neither wanted nor was permitted to do by our instructors.

On some level, I understood that this was safe, but I still kept thinking, *I don't get it. Do you push with your legs? How do you hold the rope? When you go over the edge of the cliff, do you adjust your body? How does this work? Because, I, the twelve-year old in the body of adult Ken Schneck, don't get it!*

Seeing me panicking, the woman who was slated to go eighth offered me her spot. At first, I declined, but then I suddenly changed my mind as I didn't think I could wait another minute. I accepted her offer, thanked her, stepped forward, and one of our instructors clipped the ropes to my harness. With that audible *click* of the metal, my anxiety skyrocketed. I still didn't understand how repelling worked and that led me right to the place where I decided, *No. No, I can't do this.*

This wasn't hesitation. This wasn't reluctance. This was me, really feeling in that moment that I could not actually walk off that cliff.

I told my instructor I might have to bail on this activity. She tried to explain it more. I reiterated that I might have to bail on this activity. She kept trying to explain it more. I looked at her desperately, but even as I was looking at her desperately, I was backing up to the cliff. I still didn't get it, but I thought maybe the mechanics would just fall into place.

They did.

And they didn't.

Once my feet were on the edge of the cliff, I looked at the supportive face of the instructor and I pushed off. It immediately didn't feel right. I emotionally felt off balance, physically fell off balance, and my whole body crunched against the side of the cliff. I scraped up my right elbow and my right pinky finger, but I soldiered down. I truly hated the experience and I was adrift in a bottomless pit of negativity. The whole process felt wrong and jerky. I still kept thinking that I couldn't figure out how the process worked even after my feet touched the ground. I felt really annoyed and unbelievably embarrassed; I was convinced I had messed up repelling.

Karen, our main trip leader/guide/guru, immediately challenged me as she unhooked the ropes from my harness. She pointedly asked why I looked so visibly annoyed and upset after having just completed my first-ever repel off a cliff. I struggled to come up with an answer; I couldn't put it into words, which is usually not a huge issue for me. What was my problem?

My only goal was to make it to the bottom of the cliff. Which I did. So why was I in such a negative state? And it wasn't just a negative state: I really and truly felt lost in disappointment. I should have felt exponentially more proud (or, at least, at a similar level) repelling off of a cliff as I did crossing that river a few short hours ago.

I just couldn't get out of my own head after the cliff and I was anxious for the day to end. I mumbled something to Karen about not understanding the mechanics of what I had just done, and she took the time to draw a picture and explain it. After her explanation, she said, "You may or may not get how this works, and the look in your eyes says that you don't, but you know that's not actually why you're frustrated, right?" I knew right in that moment that I had quite a few days ahead of me with Karen and my own process of growth.

Tomorrow, we move into the backpacking part of the trip as we will be setting out into the backcountry of this area of the Colorado Rocky Mountains. I was pretty dark and stormy the rest of today and I knew that my backpack would feel infinitely heavier if I didn't somehow return my body, mind, and overall energy into that place of feeling proud and accomplished. As I'm about to shut my eyes and get some sleep, I know that I need to get back there and I need to get back there quickly. I crossed a river. I repelled off a cliff. I should feel different.

Day 4
June 17, 2015

Huge, enormous, earthshattering news alert: I got my trail name yesterday.

Hugely upsetting, enormously depressing, earthclouding news alert: My trail name is Kitty.

Kitty.

And there's nothing I can do about it. I'm trying to accept the name assigned to me with the grace with which it was given. And by that I mean, my protests fell on deaf ears and only served to cement the fact that my trail name is Kitty.

Kitty's origin story goes like this: after I completed the repel yesterday, I had ink on my hands from gripping the rope so tightly as I fumbled down the side of the cliff. I must have touched my face to wipe away some sweat when Karen was explaining the mechanics of repelling. I turned to face the group and Llama remarked that I had a black smudge under my nose that evoked the facial hair of a certain German dictator. Quickly fearing that my trail name would somehow be connected to fascism, I licked the back of my hand (again, ink covered the front of my hand) and attempted to remove the smudge. Such was my aversion to this anti-Semitic association that I did this action of licking the back of my hand and wiping my face several times in quick succession. Suddenly, the association shifted from World War II fascist to a preening feline.

Llama yelled out, "Kitty! His trail name is Kitty!" and everyone quickly exclaimed, "Kitty!" And that was that. Seriously: Kitty. My earlier excitement and zeal to have my own trail name diminished considerably in that moment.

Today was our first real day of backpacking. Before coming on this trip, I very stupidly watched the movie *Wild*, which really is not the best preparation for your first-ever backpacking trip. I laid out all of my items this morning and couldn't stop my mind from flashing to the scene in which Reese Witherspoon struggled to fit all of her items into her pack and then fell down when she finally maneuvered the pack onto her shoulders.

Although technically I didn't fall down, I wasn't that far from it. Holy hell, that pack was heavy. In addition to my own items, I had to carry my portion of the group gear: a huge sack of food with the heaviest Fig Newtons ever made in the history of Fig Newtons, all of the metal tarp stakes for all of the tarps for the entire group, one of the enormous three tarps for the whole group, and a ton of other items too multiple and random to name. It never occurred to me that we would have to carry so much group gear in addition to our own items. It's not that I thought someone else would carry the gear for us. I just hadn't thought about it at all. More important, when did Fig Newtons get so heavy?

We all piled into a van, arrived at the trailhead, unloaded all of our gear, and wistfully watched the van pull away. So this was it. We were going to be backpacking for real and it started right at that moment. We only had around five miles to hike today, but they were five miles straight up, so it was a bit rough. Suddenly, there were mossy rills and untouched snow and stunning mountain vistas, all of which were truly breathtaking. They felt even more breathtaking given that I'm not usually someone whose breath is taken away by such things. They also felt truly breathtaking because of that outdoorsy equation of what happens when you multiply altitude by physical exertion.

Sometime around midday, I was functioning as the Sweep: he who stays at the back and ensures that nothing is left behind, be it straggling backpacker or microtrash (a new word for me and one I feel like I can use as a really effective metaphor). As much as we were empowered with different roles (Sweep, Leader, Compass Reader, etc.), we always had the safety net of the three Outward Bound staff members who would be accompanying us: Karen (our sage, grounding guide), Lauren (our ethereal sprite of a leader who talked me over that cliff), and Mark (our boundless ball of energy who regularly and convincingly told us we could do anything).

In my role as Sweep, I was joined at the back of the pack by Karen, our main leader. Karen is everything you could ever want in a leader on a journey like this and quite a bit more than everything for which you could ever hope. I instantly respected her and most certainly wanted to be her. She is wise, a little snarky, and sports a resume boasting decades and decades of leading these trips. Karen is a woman always ready to answer your question with the rejoinder of, "You tell me."

In other circumstances, Karen would represent everything that would get on my last nerve. We would ask her, "Where on this map are we, Karen?" and she would immediately reply, "We are wherever we are."

Back in Cleveland, I would probably then think, *That's not what I fucking meant!* but here on a trail in the Colorado Rocky Mountains I thought, *Yes. Yes, Karen. You're totally right.*

We would ask her, "Karen, what time is the van picking us up on Sunday" and she would immediately reply, "It's Wednesday. Not Sunday."

Back in Cleveland, I would probably then think, *That's not what I fucking meant!* but here on a trail in the Colorado Rocky Mountains, I thought, *Yes. Yes, Karen. You're totally right.*

I clearly am a Karen convert.

At the rear of the pack and without preamble, Karen suddenly went right in on me, continuing yesterday's exchange from the bottom of the cliff after my repelling debacle. After interacting with me for two days, she was able to conclude that I'm not kind to myself (I'm not), that I carry my scars around with me right on the surface (I do), and that I don't seem to let go of past experiences where I feel I have failed (somebody get this lady a lifetime supply of turtle wax for winning this round!). She concluded that I really needed to pause and look around and figure out where I was. I started to respond with something either witty, irreverent, or distracting, but she silenced me and urged me to pause, look around, and figure out where I was.

For once, I actually listened to the support that was being offered to me. The enormity of the situation suddenly crashed into me. I wasn't in the protected setting of Esalen, or the controlled schedule of Uganda, or pedaling all those miles straight ahead unencumbered on my bike. I was in the middle of the Colorado Rocky Mountains with no sense of where I was headed, carrying a really heavy pack, and pushing myself so far out of my comfort zone with zero opportunity to retreat. It was that last part that really rammed things home. At Esalen, I ran from the room when I needed a break. In Uganda, I stepped away from the group and wandered around the school grounds when I needed a break. On the AIDS ride, I pulled off to the side of the road and stopped pedaling when I needed a break. Here in the Colorado Rocky Mountains, I really couldn't step away and retreat. And why would I want to? I was having an amazing conversation with an amazing woman in an amazing setting.

The big takeaway from that dialogue was centered on the idea of past failures. I've been trying desperately to work through some particularly painful parts of my past (*see: Divorce, Ken's*) for so many years, but she highlighted another option: stop talking about it to others for a long period of time. If each telling feels like a knife wound, what if I moved on to other narratives and told different stories? What if I stopped unsheathing the dagger? What if I just focused on new and distinctly happier tales?

Karen was in no way saying that this shift would erase either the facts of my past or the accompanying pain; she was merely suggesting that I seemed to be going out of my way to inflict self-damage when, in fact, there were so many other stories to tell . . . positive stories even! Case in point: forget the part where I scraped up my body and didn't understand the mechanics of the process of repelling. Instead, why not focus on the part where I repelled off a fucking cliff? Focusing on the positive would most certainly take some practice, but I was intrigued, and that's always a good first step toward change for me.

The rest of the day was marginally easier, if only because I was lost in this idea of a paradigm shift. When I finally set up camp, I didn't feel so overwhelmed. When I finally pooped in the woods, I didn't feel so overwhelmed. When I finally chose three people with whom I would share a tarp for the first night in my life actually sleeping in the wilderness, I didn't feel so overwhelmed. Everything certainly feels huge, unfamiliar, and full of meaning. But I feel present.

Regarding that last detail about tarp mates, I shared a sleeping space with Llama, Canon, and Raven (it's trail names from here on out, folks). We called our parcel of land "Christmas Village," because all of our socks were airing out on a tree like stockings by the chimney. The vibe felt jovial, familiar, and supportive. All of a sudden, this Kitty was feeling pretty darn good. Yay! Kitty!

Day 5
June 18, 2015

Today was wretchedly, horribly, breathtakingly painful. I remember penning a similar start to an entry years ago on my first trip to Uganda in which I noted that I wasn't referring to physical pain. Here in Colorado, I am casting metaphors aside and am talking about a physical pain that is completely derailing my experience.

In preparing for this trip back in Cleveland, I had been thoroughly freaked out by Laura, my backpacking-savvy friend, who expressed real and valid worry and concern about my lack of preparedness for the physical piece of this trip, even as she tried to settle my mind by sending me John Muir memes. Consequently, in the week leading up to this trip, I upped my workout routine dramatically. Too dramatically, it would seem. Somewhere in the walking of the many miles in the Cuyahoga Valley National Park, the biking of various trails, the sporadic tennis matches, and the almost daily trips to the cardio equipment in my campus' gym, I tweaked my hip.

To make matters worse, I have learned in the past twenty-four hours that the word "backpack" is wholly misleading; although the insanely heavy pack looks like it is resting on your back, the weight is, in actuality, resting on your hips. Anyone who has ever previously gone backpacking would read that last bit and immediately respond, "Duh." Please keep in mind that the "Previously Gone Backpacking" group is a demographic with which I neither have an active membership nor even a remote affiliation. This was news to me.

The pain in my hip had been a pretty sharp ache the first few days of this journey, but the past few days with that backpack weight on my hips, the amount of pain I was experiencing has exponentially increased. We're talking epic levels of pain here. This morning, while lying down under the tarp in Christmas Village, I attempted to change out of the gym shorts I wore to sleep and into my hiking pants. The pain level was high. Very high. As in, I actually screamed out in pain because it hurt so badly. Thankfully, Llama, Canon, and Raven were all away from the tarp so no one heard me yell. Though no one was around to hear it, I assure you: this gay-Jew-tree falling down on the ground most certainly *did* make noise. And not only did I yelp, but that action of simply getting changed really and truly did take every ounce of determination that I could muster.

Now this was a huge predicament for me. On one hand, I was in a ton of pain. I didn't know what was wrong with me but this was not me aggravating a pre-existing injury. This was something new and acute and I wasn't sure what I could do to make it better (or, at least, keep it from getting worse). I even tried just stretching up to the sky in some sort of yoga sun pose that I think is supposed to infuse your body with the healing rays of the morning sun or something else that I don't know because I've never taken a non-Bikram yoga class in my life. I'm not sure whether my chakra was off or my chi was skewed, but there was no healing to be found with that stretch; instead, I experienced a ton more pain.

On the other hand, here I am in the backcountry of the Colorado Rocky Mountains on an eight-day adventure. It wasn't that I couldn't quit, as I have zero doubt that there was some evacuation plan that could extricate an ailing individual from the trip with both equal parts efficacy and embarrassment for he who would have to leave. Sure, I knew that I could somehow leave but I was overwhelmed with the idea of this trip being "the likes of which I will never see again." Colorado felt all kinds of once-in-a-lifetime and my stubbornness (and aversion to anything that might embarrass me) trumped my pain urging me toward a decision to abandon this experience.

Did I leave? Absolutely not. Was I paying attention to what was going on around me? Absolutely not. Today's skill-based activity was orienteering: the process of using a map and compass to triangulate direction using landmarks in an unfamiliar terrain. Let's be clear here: on my best, pain-free, living-in-my-comfort-zone day, orienteering would have been a bear for me. My brain is simply not wired to use a map and a compass to triangulate direction using landmarks in an unfamiliar terrain. Add in the physical pain to my state of being, and my brain rejected even saying the word "orienteering," much less actually trying to engage in the practice.

As far as hip pain goes, orienteering sucks. If you're trying to forget hip pain by throwing yourself into moving forward at a regular pace and letting your mind go numb, orienteering—with its requirement that you stop every six inches or so to "shoot a new bearing"—is truly horrible. If you're someone who really enjoys wavy lines, and what they can come to represent on a map, and how the distance between those wavy lines can correspond to how you're using a compass, and putting "Red Fred in the Shed" after you adjust the compass to compensate for some multiplier that exists in fine print at the bottom of the map, then orienteering is just the best. Also, if that's you, we're probably not friends. But for me, on this day, orienteering sucked and I could not have cared less if Red fucking Fred could find his fucking shed.

As you can see, there was no way for my physical state to not be affecting my emotional state. I may have tried in the morning to let a spirit of adventure dominate my being, but the pain was getting worse. So too was my attitude. Any attempts to control my sourness went from halfhearted to nonexistent as the hours and the unending starting and stopping progressed.

It was thus that I lost it at one point and snapped at my trip-mates. The trails on which we are traversing have been extraordinarily narrow and the only way to cover much of the ground before us is for our group to hike in a single-file formation. A single-file formation means that when one person stops, so too must everyone behind them. Today, I again assumed the role of Sweep in the back of the pack. Yes, the starting and stopping is annoying and even more so for me today given the pain, but it's so embedded as a part of this experience that to get upset at every hiking halt would be to truly throw myself into lunacy.

So, fine. I knew we were going to stop a ton, but my frustration came from my tripmates ahead of me stopping to consult the compass and not looking back to see where that left the rest of us behind them. Yes, we would be stopping too, but what was the terrain under our feet during the break in the action? At one point, one of these stops literally had me straddling a log with my right foot on one side of the log in the snow and my left foot on the other side of the log on a muddy, slippery incline. As I couldn't get mad at my hip, I instead became incensed with the individuals who called for that particular pause.

When we all gathered a few minutes later in a clearing for a water break, I snapped at everyone out front orienteering. I curtly told them that they actually needed to look behind them to see where everyone was standing and devise a system to check in to make sure everyone felt like they were on solid footing before executing a break in the forward momentum. Those leading orienteering immediately agreed because I had a good point, but my delivery was so fucked up in its palpable annoyance and condescension, it made for a truly uncomfortable water break. I mumbled an apology for my tone, but I was so embarrassed at how I handled the situation that I broke off from the team dynamic for most of the remaining day.

I was only half-listening when the denizens of Christmas Village told me that there was some drama about figuring out exactly where we were supposed to end up at the end of the day. Apparently, the leaders had been questioning whether there even *was* some place specific at which we were supposed to end up at the end of the day. At this point in the trip, we all knew those weren't questions Karen was going to answer with any specificity. There was some squabbling amongst tripmates as to where we were trying to reach and then, when we reached a clearing, if we even had arrived there, wherever there was. With daylight dwindling, a decision was made that, yes, this was indeed our intended destination.

We set up Christmas Village, hung our stockings by tree-trunk chimneys with care, and I heard about some tiffs that were had when individuals' leadership styles conflicted and, apparently, prevented us from reaching our destination earlier in the day. But, again, I was only half-listening. This was not a good day and I had called it quits in that clearing where I had snapped verbally at my tripmates.

Tomorrow is a big day. We are summiting a mountain, which is apparently not a metaphor either. Were all of my regularly used idioms real? Just to be sure, I checked in with Karen. She assured me that it wasn't a mental exercise. It would be an actual summiting of a mountain.

Then, after we descend from the summit, we will set out for our solo night during which your sleeping arrangements cannot be anywhere in view of anyone else's sleeping arrangements. Currently, I don't have a handle on sleeping in the wilderness, and this is when I'm in Christmas Village surrounded by three supportive women. Tomorrow, I would have to set up my tent and sleep alone. And even as the enormity of tomorrow's agenda was crashing down on me as I close out this day, I am convinced that tomorrow will be better than today. It kinda has to be.

Day 6
June 19, 2015

Today I climbed my first mountain: a trek that took me to an actual summit.

Also, today I had a breakdown: an all-out, tears-streaming-down-my-cheeks crying mess.

I have been obsessing for hours now about the order in which to put those two events. That's ridiculous, right? I climbed a fucking mountain! How do you not put reaching the summit of an 11,300-foot mountain before any other instance of anything? The order of any day should always be:

1. I climbed a mountain.
2. Other stuff.

But the fact that the mountain narrowly—and we're talking the slimmest of margins here—beat out my crying, well that's a testament to just how all-over-the-place I am here at the end of this colossal day that has concluded with my lying here in isolation. But first, let's recap the events of the day that led me to this solitary place.

Last night ended in a most unexpected way. If you read yesterday's entry or even put your fingers over the words, the physical pain, the defeatist attitude, and the overall negativity would have had anyone concluding, "Yeah, not a good day for Ken." Then a Christmas miracle happened. Sometime around 8:00 p.m., when we would normally be bedding down in Christmas Village for the night, our entire group (twelve weary participants and three endlessly upbeat staff) ended up sitting in a circle in a glowing field of yellow glacier lilies. Now, I have absolutely no knowledge of flora, so I have no clue whether the "yellow" is redundant or if glacier lilies come in myriad hues and shades. Regardless, there we were, sitting in a circle in a glowing field of yellow glacier lilies.

Someone asked whether I could show the entire group a game I had played with six of them yesterday morning when we were waiting for everyone to gather their belongings after breakfast. It was one of my old establish-and-maintain-a-pattern theater games derived from days directing a student health education drama group called HEAT (Health Education/Awareness Theater). That was one of the better acronyms I have created in life as the students in the troupe got to run around campus yelling, "I'm in HEAT! I'm in HEAT!" Everyone won.

Mind you, I have played this particular improv game countless times over the years, including as a focusing exercise when my graduate students come to class with particularly unfocused energy. At this point in my life with this particular exercise, I have an established and well-worn facilitation script in my head that really doesn't take too much energy, intentionality, or presence to recite. This is not to say that I sound robotic or disengaged, but I also don't have to be 100 percent present to make the activity come to pass.

Except with the group in this circle.

This group was different.

This circle of fifteen Outward Bounders were so attentive, so eager, and so upbeat that they brought all of my attention into focus. To give them any fraction less than 100 percent presence felt acutely dishonorable. I switched on my entertaining-teacher-supporter switch and it all just worked. They played the game with fervency, enthusiastically leaning in when they were creating overlapping patterns of words, and genuinely seeking my insight when they made a mistake that prevented them from being more successful at their patternmaking.

This was yet another experience I needed in my life that I didn't know I needed until it happened. And I needed it to happen right in that moment last night. I was in an unfamiliar place with unfamiliar people doing unfamiliar activities all while I was experiencing unfamiliar pain. I needed to be good at something. I needed to *feel* good at something. This group provided that opportunity as well as that reinforcement in spades. I went to sleep so infinitely more content than I ever could have imagined when I penned yesterday's dour-dosed entry.

This morning, we ate a quick breakfast as we had to scale Marble Mountain and start our descent before 11:30 a.m., so as not to be on top of a mountain during the most ferocious time of inclement weather should inclement weather occur. Everyone was excited. Visibly, demonstrably excited. Everyone knew there was a mountain to climb in front of us and people were on their toes, bouncing buoyantly as we packed our significantly lighter daypacks and started out on the trail.

Every day of our backcountry Outward Bound experience, three members of our group serve as our daily group leaders. Before we set out today, today's leaders (Llama, Raven, and Rock Rabbit), let us know that they would be functioning today more as guides than as leaders. They instructed us to take the lead of the group if we ever felt the urge or to hang back toward the rear of the pack if that was our inclination. Today, they told us, was all about focusing our individual energy into the group, rather than directing it toward three members of our group at the front of the pack. The goal was to be one big happy family.

Only, we weren't one big happy family. This should come as no surprise to (a) anyone who has ever studied group dynamics, (b) anyone who has ever read about organizational behavior, or (c) anyone who has ever spent a few days around, y'know, people. One of our twelve has caused friction. If she has a trail name, I don't know what it is, so let's call her No Trail Name Lady. So much of our family dysfunction seems to have localized on her presence.

No Trail Name Lady is not in good physical shape for this trip. Like, at all. This is not Snarky Ken being critical or body shaming or anything of the sort. This has been the group's lived reality for days. The frustration that has arisen is not on the fact of her limitations; on the contrary, these limitations were understood, as she just had a baby a few months ago and it sounded like she has had a horror of a year emotionally. The frustration that has arisen is solely focused on the effects of her physicality. As a group, we have to stop to take breaks to accommodate No Trail Name Lady more than you can ever possibly imagine.

In preparing for this Outward Bound experience, I was told to prep for hikes of twelve to seventeen miles a day. In actuality, these past few days we have clocked in maybe three or four miles a day, tops. Now, some of that decreased mileage is due to both the skills and activities laid out before us (repelling, orienteering with the compasses, map reading, etc.) as well as a very tricky terrain under our boots. But it is also undeniable that a huge chunk of our much-shortened mileage is due to No Trail Name Lady.

This has been a source of supreme irritation for members of our group, particularly those who signed up specifically because they wanted to cover twelve to seventeen miles a day. I, Ken Schneck, was again in a tricky spot. On the one hand, the constant rest breaks are maddening. Really and truly maddening. On the other hand, my hip really, really hurts, so the decreased mileage has made the hiking immeasurably more doable for me.

Complicating matters, there was the part where No Trail Name Lady wasn't exactly the rosiest participant on the trip. To be fair, I'm not sure what level of rosiness would have mitigated the feelings of frustration a huge chunk of our group was experiencing due to her rest breaks. But I feel pretty confident concluding that she was significantly far away from whatever level it was that would have mitigated the feelings of frustration that a huge chunk of our group was experiencing. Also, to be honest and upfront here, the residents of Christmas Village got a teensy bit Mean Girls about the whole situation. I'm not super proud of that.

Case in point: a few days ago at base camp, when we were laying out our belongings for the staff to check over to make sure we weren't carrying an ounce more weight in our backpacks than we absolutely needed, No Trail Name Lady discovered that she had forgotten an essential outer layer of clothing. I had actually brought an extra outer layer: a brand-new hoodie I was excited to wear but didn't really *need*, per se. So I happily handed it over to No Trail Name Lady.

For days out in the backcountry, No Trail Name Lady made comments about being cold but she never put on the hoodie I gave her. For my part, I simply could not bring myself to say, "Hey, what about that hoodie I gave you?" This morning, from across the camp, I saw Scribe—a tripmate who could have easily been an Outward Bound staff member given her outdoor expertise—walking around camp holding out my hoodie to different members of our group. When she finally got to me, she asked, "Is this yours?" I said that it was and asked her where she got it. She replied that No Trail Name Lady gave it to her because she couldn't remember whose hoodie it was and she didn't feel like carrying it around anymore. No Trail Name Lady wanted her pack to be lighter.

I was incensed.

First, how do you not remember who gave you a brand-new hoodie three days ago when you needed something you didn't have? But, fine, those days were blurry. Far more important, even with the close-to-zero knowledge that I possess about backpacking, I do know with certainty that what you carry out into the wilderness is what you carry back in. You don't start unloading some of your items on Day 5 when you're out in the middle of nowhere.

I went back to Christmas Village and word-vomited this story on Llama, Raven, and Canon. We were chattering away angrily about the whole situation and somehow landed on the refrain, "Don't poop in the hoodie" as a code for venting frustration about No Trail Name Lady. It was childish; it was petty; it was high school. And it was where I was at that moment.

With this undercurrent of *My-So-Called-Colorado-Life* angst, we needed the "Teamwork Makes the Dream Work" framework for the day that our leaders had set up for us. We needed something we could all accomplish together that had a very real element of physicality to it, not just sitting down in a circle playing a theater game. We needed to coalesce as a group or the next few days were going to be hell.

With all of this backstory in hand, we bounded up that trail toward the summit. The positive energy was so infectious that Ken Schneck took the lead of the pack for the first time this whole expedition. And lest you be confused, there was only one Ken Schneck in our group and that Ken Schneck was indeed me. Looking back on this morning, I couldn't pinpoint exactly what propelled me to the front of the pack. I felt the energy pushing me forward and, instead of falling back on my normal routine of resistance, I not only embraced this positive spirit, but I embraced it with gusto.

Please know that I wasn't some silent front-of-the-pack kind of guy. Oh no, dear reader, I was a lively, jubilant, bellowing front-of-the-pack kind of guy. But instead of bellowing incredible words of encouragement or sage John Muir aphorisms, instead, I bellowed "Down by the Bay" as we climbed. For those of you readers who are, like some of my tripmates, unfamiliar with this childhood song, I truly mourn for your upbringing. No one should be denied the opportunity to supply a rhyming couplet of an animal doing something nutty ("Have you ever seen a llama, wearing pajamas?" or "Have you ever seen a whale, with a polka-dotted tail?"). It took more instruction than I ever could have anticipated, but everyone in our pack line eventually got the hang of "Down by the Bay." Up we went. I sang. I smiled. I ascended.

Right after the "Down by the Bay" chorale concert had concluded, we reached a section of the trail that had disappeared due to a recent snowfall. It quickly became clear that we needed to plot a new way up to the summit, so the group rested on a sloped patch of land on the mountainside, while our leaders and the Outward Bound staff formed a new plan.

I stood on a rock, faced away from our mountain, and looked out at the majestic vista before me. We had already climbed quite a bit this morning and our initial elevation when we set out was pretty high up to start, with so I had a lot of land out in front of me upon which I could let my eyes drink in. Also, I had a lot of land below me upon which I could let my eyes drink in. And I think it was the idea of "below me" that started the process of the wheels coming off the van of Ken's composure.

I started getting anxious. Really anxious. The surroundings were epic: purple mountain majesties everywhere you looked. The questions that started assaulting my brain felt just as epic: *How high up are we at this point? How much farther do we have to scale? What is the terrain like? Can I conceivably fall off this mountain and die? Seriously, what the fuck am I doing here? Why do I sign up for things like this? How can I possibly think that things like this are things that I can do? Also, can I conceivably fall off this mountain and die?*

I knew that I had to sit down, but that simple action was something I was hesitant to do because it was, y'know, a mountainside. I understood how to walk up a trail and down a trail. In that moment, I couldn't understand how I could possibly sit down on a rock on a mountainside. Much like the repelling, the mechanics were out of my grasp. In this case, the mechanics of sitting down.

A voice deep down from the bottom of my soul came up the top of my head and reminded me that I had sat down on rocks at other times in my life. Countless times, in fact. I slowly and gingerly lowered my body down on that rock, a bit away from the rest of the group. I just stared out. We had borne witness to these stunning panoramas for many days now, but this was the first time that I looked out at them and felt like an insignificant speck. Any self-importance or talent-based ego that I had ever felt in my life was washed away. I felt like nothing.

191

From behind me, I heard Karen instruct the group that we needed to put on our helmets because there was unknown and unsure terrain ahead. At breakfast, the other two Outward Bound staff members had said that we wouldn't need to don our helmets during this climb. Karen was now telling us that we had to put on our helmets. Was I going to die? I couldn't stop questioning whether I was going to die. Karen said we had to put on our helmets. Clearly this meant that I could die.

Princess Podiatry, a tripmate who was amazing at footcare, walked over to where I was gingerly perched and asked me how I was doing. I was the recipient of this question a lot during the trip due to the known fact that I had never before been camping. I always did my best to be positive because I was embarrassed at my lack of experience and determined (read: stubborn) to make it through Outward Bound successfully. But that was all before Karen told us to put on our helmets, which had no other translation in my head other than, *You could die*. Without thinking, I told Princess Podiatry, "I think I want to go back down now."

Then I started crying.

Here's the thing about me and crying: I honestly don't do it that much. During emotional cinematic moments, I get choked up, but I don't cry. When my beloved grandmother Alice died a few years ago, I felt sorrow and a constant tightness in my chest, but I didn't cry. When my ex-husband sent me that email last year telling me he had put down our dog with whom I shared a bed for seven years, I lamented and couldn't stop sighing deeply, but I didn't cry. Crying is just not the way I normally express myself.

But there, sitting on that rock on the side of Marble Mountain in the Colorado Rocky Mountain range? I was crying. Tears were steadily flowing, originating from under my sunglasses and running downstream down my cheeks. I wasn't sobbing or gasping; I was just sitting there, unmoving, with a salty river dampening my entire visage.

Karen walked over to my rock. I think maybe Princess Podiatry had beckoned her over, but I'm not sure about that. Karen softly told me that the rest of the climb was completely optional. She also told me that she has been leading these expeditions for thirty-two years and, based on her extensive experience, she knew I could do this. Princess Podiatry put her arm around me and told me that I could do this. I was not telling myself I could do this. I just sat and stared out as I couldn't bring myself to look at either woman. I kept on crying: unmoving and perfectly still, yet crying.

What was happening? Four minutes ago—really and truly four minutes ago—I was out in front of the group. I was singing. I was bouncing. I was feeling everything I wanted to feel on this trip. Now, all I wanted to do was escape this mountain, but I could not for the life of me plot a viable escape route. I could not slow my brain and I certainly could not get out of my own way. I had no idea how I was even going to get up from that rock, either to escape or to continue the climb. I was yet again frozen.

From behind me, I heard someone ask No Trail Name Lady how she was doing. She also got this question a lot during the trip. Her answers were always some variation of an observation of how hard this all was. That is, if she even answered at all. Sometimes her focus was so intense that she didn't even acknowledge the question. Or if she did acknowledge it on some level, she didn't respond verbally. This time, she had an answer and it was one that changed my day.

"I'm just as scared as Kent."

With her short answer, my attention not only shifted, but shifted seismically. Instead of planning an escape route, the only thing running through my head was the eternal question of, *What. The. Fuck?* Those three words chased out pretty much every thought I was having on so many different levels.

First off, it's *Ken.* My name is Ken. Seriously? It's Day 5. Why the fuck do you not know my name? Remember that time I gave you that hoodie that you never wore and that other time I spent five days with you backpacking in the Colorado Rocky Mountains? I not only know your name but I also know the weird-ass way you spell it, which is either an affect that you adopted at one point to be different, or it's a curse given to you by nefarious parents who thought, *Let's put in a 'Y' where no 'Y' was ever meant to go.* Do you seriously not know my name? Why the fuck do you not know my name?

Second, and far more important, I was livid that she verbally stuck us together as birds of a feather. I didn't feel we were and I was totally pissed off at the association. This wasn't about my not wanting to associate with her, as I was obviously struggling as well; I was so angry because I felt like she had thrown me under the bus to make herself feel better about her own struggles. She had no idea what was going on in my head and it felt like a cheap shot compounded by her misnaming me.

The crazy part was, as I was livid, pissed off, and angry, I found myself getting up from that rock to climb the rest of the mountain. I am not saying that this rage was the healthiest motivation to get me up off of that rock, but it effectively unfroze me when I couldn't find a way out. I put my hiking poles in front of me, took smaller steps, dug in the heels of my perfectly contoured boots (shout out, Asolo!), and began to climb with the rest of the group.

Look, the climb was scary. And I am certainly not asserting that petty anger (and even these few hours later, I could see just how petty it was) was the only thing making me put one foot in front of the other. Honestly, I can't pinpoint exactly what propelled me to the summit.

But I got there.

I was standing on the summit of a mountain. The mood around me was celebratory. I was a thing apart from the revelry. After some group picture taking and the devouring of a gift of dark chocolate M&Ms the Outward Bound staff gifted us for reaching the summit, the group panned out across the summit of Marble Mountain for some solo reflection time. The view was almost impossible to believe and there really was a part of me that was appreciative of the experience. At the same time, I also really wanted to climb down and was slightly anxious for what descent would actually be like for me.

The group circled back up and was asked to share something they learned on the climb that made them a stronger person. People shared stories of loss that brought them to tears on that mountaintop. Others shared insights of newfound fortitude. Someone else told a bawdy, but on-point tale of a previous climb.

I shared nothing. I stayed silent. All I kept thinking about was how I had been crying. Yet again, I had accomplished the climb. I had done what I set out to do. I had reached the summit of an actual, nonmetaphorical mountain. But I was fixated on my own perception of my failure. I was right back on the bottom of that cliff after the repelling experience. There on the summit of an actual mountain, I somehow didn't have the strength to share in that moment.

We started the climb down and I was near the front of the pack behind Llama, Raven, Canon, and Princess Podiatry. My footing felt sure. My steps felt secure. I was feeling great even if "great" in this instance was a bit relative. I wasn't frozen on a rock crying, and that felt great.

Behind me was No Trail Name Lady. She repeatedly admonished us to slow down and take more rest breaks. At least, she either admonished us or that's how we heard her. I wasn't sure which was true at that point. Regardless, we sorta listened and slowed down. But we also sorta didn't, which then triggered more admonishments.

At one point, Llama and I rewrote the lyrics to "Part of Your World" from the *The Little Mermaid* to reflect the slow pace. It was childish; it was petty; it was high school. And it was where I was in that moment. The lyrics really were terrible though. I knew I could do better.

When we had completed around 75 percent of our descent, we reached an avalanche pass covered in snow. Two of the Outward Bound staff tested it and determined it was safe for some activity whose name I can't quite remember, but translates into lying on your back and sliding down the chute, luge-style, without the luge. Those who wanted to complete the descent via this method could pass on their poles to those who wanted to walk the rest of the way down the mountain.

I decided to walk down the rest of the mountain. The body sliding really did look fun and as someone who really enjoys similar experiences at water parks, this would normally be something I would race out front to do. But at the same time, I had reached my capacity for new things for today. I really was done with the mountain and couldn't add another activity. With arms full of our tripmates' hiking poles, I walked the rest of the way down the mountain with Karen and Canon. To her great credit, No Trail Name Lady slid down the avalanche pass.

We three hikers arrived at camp around twenty minutes before the rest of the group, as their human sliding emptied them out onto a different trail about a half-mile from our camp. We had barely dropped everyone's poles on the ground before Karen turned to me and started in. She began by noting how great it was to see my energy at facilitating the theater game the night before. But, she continued, that was only a part of me. She said there was a different part of me that I showed on the rock on that mountainside, a human part that I clearly lock up away from prying eyes.

Karen took off her sunglasses and I saw that there were tears in her eyes. This then triggered tears in my eyes. I can't remember exactly what she said next, and I really wish I could because I would play it every morning for the rest of my life. The gist was that I needed to express myself more as a whole person, not just one who can teach and entertain and distract, but one who cries, one who needs help, and one who lets other people see all of that.

I actually had to put my head down for a second after penning that last sentence.

It was a lot to take in. Not all of it was unfamiliar as it echoed much of what Mary said at Esalen, but the experience of climbing the mountain certainly changed the context. All I could do was thank Karen and try to process the gift of words, sentiments, and emotion she had given me.

The second half of the day was spent prepping for our solo night. As I understood it, you set up your own solo tarp out of view from the rest of your tripmates and exist by yourself until a staff member comes to get you in the morning. We split up into groups to scout a spot to set up; Llama, Raven, and I walked with Karen to find a choice piece of land. My chief concern was finding a spot with two trees to serve as solid anchors to my more-than-shoddy tarp assembling skills. I located exactly what I was looking for, but Karen pointed out that we could catch a glimpse of Llama's blue tarp through the trees, so I had to find a new spot. I finally landed in a heavily wooded area with downed trees all around me.

My tarp assembly was not only bad, it was even worse than I thought it would be. All of the knot-tying skills I had learned and executed over the past few days in Christmas Village were suddenly wiped from my mind. What the hell? I knew how to tie these knots. I had tied them over and over. And now I couldn't remember a single thing. We were told we could use two stakes to aid in our assembly if we really needed to. There was certainly some discouragement that lived in the phrase "if we really needed to," but I quickly bypassed any such discouragement and grabbed some stakes with zero hesitation.

The resulting structure evoked the vague suggestion of a shelter with distinct notes of both determination and a strong bouquet of ineptitude. It was too high off the ground and the knots were less secure and more shoelace-esque. But it is the shelter I made and I immediately and inexplicably assumed the same level of pride my mother displayed when I presented her with a horrid turquoise, ivory, and black macramé wall hanging that I made in sleepaway camp. Much to my confusion, that wall hanging never actually made it to hang on a wall.

So here I sit, with daylight fading, wrapping up this long entry under my tarp. It definitely just hit me that I am by myself in the woods. The whistle around my neck could bring help within seconds, but I know that I won't be needing it. What I need is solo time and here I have it.

I just keep thinking: *I climbed a mountain today. And I cried.* I've struggled all day with how to order those two milestones. Ultimately, I have come to understand that, no matter which one I write first, they cannot live independently of each other. They are tied together. They exist on the same page. To have one eclipse the other would be to deny the totality and enormity of today's experience of summits, be it the climbing to the top of a mountain or simply standing up from a rock.

Day 7
June 20, 2015

Sometimes stuff happens in a day and you can't quite believe it all went down in the same day. Surely some space-time continuum had to have been breached for such highs and lows to all be in the same waking span. Today was most certainly one of those days.

I woke up feeling great. Not physically great. Not sure if I mentioned, but my hip hurts and hurts pretty bad. I ignored the pain yesterday, as there was so much in front of me to summit, but the pain came roaring back this morning. I'm doing my best to ignore the pain because emotionally and spiritually (a word I neither use often, nor embody), I really did feel great. The solo night was productive on so many levels and I felt appreciative.

A staff member came to retrieve me from our individual solo tarp sites and I silently walked into the center of that field of yellow glacier lilies. Everyone seemed to come in from a different direction to come together to form a circle in the middle of that field. It could not have been a more literal interpretation of individuals coming together from different paths to coalesce back into a group. It felt like the perfect start to the day. Brief words were spoken welcoming us back and we were told that we would have an opportunity to process our solo nights after breakfast.

We ate a quick breakfast, circled back up again, and began reflecting on our individual solo nights. Things got intense. Things got intense fast. Some tripmates spoke passionately about their desperate need to reconnect with nature. Others related their solo experience to their desperate need to find solitude. And others shared that their solo experience advanced their desperate need to clarify relationships with certain individuals in their lives. There was some laughter, a water basin full of tears, and a real feeling of connection in that circle.

For my part, I shared two things. First, the solo night highlighted just how much I use humor as my defense mechanism when I am uncomfortable or struggling to connect with those around me. If I can make people laugh, I can stay in their good graces. If I can make people laugh, they will notice me. If I can make people laugh, they will remember me. But sometimes, I do it at the wrong time. Last night at dinner was one of those wrong times.

Before dinner each night, we have a ritual of an evening meal circle. We start with Announcements (what's coming up for tomorrow), move on to Celebrations (kudos to others on something they might have accomplished that day), and follow that with Ownerships. Ownerships are opportunities for you to apologize and take ownership for something you might have done that day that was amiss. Then the group would conclude with a quote read by one of the leaders of the day. Rituals are an incredibly crucial practice, as they can really ground a group in a consistent activity that gathers together energy in a respectful way. Unless you are me, and you disrespect that energy.

Last night, I was anxious for solo night so I cracked a joke during Ownerships. I asked whether people should express an Ownership if they called someone else a mean name, something Canon had jokingly done to me earlier in the day. Canon smiled, told the story of the name-calling, took ownership, and a few people laughed. Before the smattering of laughter died down, Pussytoes (she who stops to greet all of her old friends, the flowers, including a flower called a pussytoe) immediately spoke up and said, "I take ownership for being annoyed when some people force others to take ownership of things." I muttered a quick apology and the group quickly moved on.

With no one for me to entertain during my solo night, my focus turned inward and my disrespectful action dominated my thinking. Thus, my first contribution to this morning's circle was to take ownership of my behavior last night. Trying to get a laugh was a selfish, shitty thing I did to upset a core ritual and I really did feel bad about it. I deserved to get called out, even as I lamented that it took that calling out to remind me that the group energy should always trump one individual desperately trying to get a cheap laugh.

The other piece I shared with the group was my own awe at how much writing I got done last night, and how proud I was of what I had penned. When I closed this journal last night, I just stared up at the tarp with my mind completely fixated on how critically important it was that I somehow find a way to replicate the circumstances that led to both my pen bleeding so much ink onto the page, as well as the true sense of satisfaction that coursed through me when the writing was complete. The desperate needs that my tripmates expressed when we went around the circle were centered, for me, on writing.

It's not like I don't set out to write when I'm at home. Many a day, I pack up my journal and walk the third of a mile to my local coffee shop (shout out, Gypsy Bean!) armed with ardent determination to pen that which would stop and make people think. I settle in, I set up my journal, I grasp my fountain pen firmly, and then something happens. I experience some fleeting thought or I don't like the person sitting next to me or I think that Jack Rocket Cat looked particularly sad when I left him just a few minutes earlier. Yes, Jack Rocket Cat always looks sad, but maybe there was some extra pang this time and he needed me to return? Without hesitation, I pack up my journal and walk the third of a mile back to my house.

There is also many a day I set out to write at home. I settle in, I set up my journal, I grasp my fountain pen firmly, and then something happens. And that something is always Netflix. Lying there on my back last night, with aching hips under a structurally unstable tarp, I was overwhelmed by the necessity of recreating the satisfaction of penning so many thoughts. It wasn't about desire. It was truly about necessity. Saying that out loud to the group helped a bit with accountability but I knew that this was a problem that was mine alone to solve when I returned to Ohio.

After the tears had dried and assorted hugs were exchanged, it was time to set out. It was my day to co-lead and I was paired with two incredible co-leaders: Princess Podiatry, she who supported me on that mountainside, and Sugar Pie, a delightful trip-mate married to an Outward Bound staff member not on our trip, a marital pressure I can't quite imagine. The three of us planned a full day of activities that would challenge our tripmates to pull together all of the different skills we were learning throughout the week and apply them to the classroom.

It was a super-short trek to our next camp, but I immediately noticed a change in the way I was hiking. My steps felt more sure. My gaze looked upward and around. Apparently, there's a great big world to see when you're not looking solely at your boots. Generally, I just experienced the sensation of being more solid. I'm not sure whether it was the artifice of being one of today's leaders or the mountain I climbed yesterday, but, today, I really felt more like me: less of an insecure, bewildered backpacker, and more the snarky gay Jew who can work through what lies before him.

After we arrived at our next camp, the group quickly set up our sleeping arrangements. I had a bit of a verbal tussle with No Trail Name Lady when she wanted to set up her tent where we had designated our kitchen to be. Then I had a follow-up verbal tussle with Princess Podiatry because she was leading No Trail Name Lady around trying to find her a new spot to sleep in, which I said was enabling but really was just me coming to the end of my patience with No Trail Name Lady. A few minutes later, I apologized to Princess Podiatry for arguing with her. She replied, "I didn't let you argue with me. I just let you vent and then made my own decisions from there." It was the most appropriate response that effectively shut me down in exactly the way I needed my negative energy to be shut down in that moment.

The group then gathered for the work we three leaders had planned. I began with an entire semester's worth of change theory delivered in twenty-five minutes. The group seemed really receptive but also anxious to try to apply some of what they learned throughout the week. We broke into small groups to devise activities around the ideas of compassion, trust, and integrity. The whole goal was to create actual deliverables for these teachers to bring back to the classroom with them. It was all going swimmingly well until Scribe dashed off, quickly leaving the group.

If you'll recall, Scribe is the tripmate who was given my hoodie by No Trail Name Lady in an attempt to find its owner. Scribe is an amazing woman. She is always the first to lend a hand, the first to ask how you are doing, and the first with an encouraging word right when you need it. She also has the look of someone experienced in this type of outdoor education work even as I struggle to write here exactly what that look looks like. When I arrived in the hotel lobby five days ago and saw how everyone was dressed, it really was Scribe's wilderness-ready apparel and energy that sent me running into that lobby bathroom to try to look more the part.

Thus, it was a jarring sight when Scribe returned to the group with tears running down her face and Karen's arm around her. Scribe, as it turned out, was suffering from a sudden case of vertigo. Our campsite was on an elevated grassy knoll, with a 360-degree view of all of the mountains around us. There was no solid backing in any direction and no tree cover under which one could seek visual refuge. The openness of the space crashed down upon Scribe and she meekly asked whether it might be possible for the group to move to another campsite just a bit up the trail. Was it a big undertaking to pack up everything we had so recently set up? Sure. Was this a no-brainer of a decision? Absolutely. There was no hesitation and it was amazing to see how the eleven of us leapt into action to support the twelfth.

That level of amazement was unbelievably uplifting. It was unbelievably inspiring. And it was unbelievably short-lived. Because as soon as we arrived at our next camp, holy shitballs, everything completely and utterly fell apart. When I write "fell apart," I really and truly mean absolute chaos. As soon as we set down our packs, everyone scattered to the four winds and any sense of group cohesion we may have had instantly evaporated.

Llama, Tripod, Raven, and Canon wanted to sleep on top of a hill, but they were told by the Outward Bound staff that they couldn't for reasons the staff wouldn't provide (we later learned it was due to a bear sighting, information I can't begin to tell you how much this non-camper really didn't want to hear). So those four tripmates were really upset. No Trail Name Lady was audibly complaining to a staff member that the group was not accommodating her pace. So she was really upset. One member of the group reflected on our abbreviated daily hiking mileage, and burst into tears as she said she didn't think she would ever have the opportunity to have this experience again, and that the opportunity she was currently experiencing was significantly truncated. So she was really upset. A group ice-breaker we played offended one of the Outward Bound staff members. So he was really upset. That then made the person who coordinated the ice-breaker really upset. And lots of other things happened. And lots of other people were really upset.

Aficionados of group dynamics would recognize the classic "storming" phase of the drama that was going down in camp. But knowing that did absolutely nothing to help me know what to do, and Karen, of course, answered all of my questions with, "What do you think you should do?" So I got really upset. I kept thinking, *I have a PhD in leading people through this group dynamics stuff!* but the distance between an advanced degree and a solution could not have felt greater than in that moment.

The energy of the group was scattered, erratic, and messy. You couldn't help but feel that some people in the group were ready to be done with the whole experience (mostly because some people actually said they were ready to be done with the whole experience). As this was our last day in the backcountry, it was difficult not to think about showers and boyfriends and technology and, yes, I was one of those people ready to be done with the whole experience.

We three leaders for the day didn't accomplish nearly what we set out to accomplish, but there was nothing we could do because we didn't anticipate the uprooting, the moving of camp, and all of the chaos that came with it. I stepped up to lead the dinner circle just so I could have some control over trying to rein in at least a fraction of that which was scattered and erratic and messy. There were various Appreciations, mostly praise for Scribe stepping up to ask whether we could move our entire camp because she was struggling, and kudos to the whole group for not hesitating in accommodating that request. There were quite a few Ownerships, apologies for earlier breakdowns and an extended Ownership from No Trail Name Lady for her slow pace even as she told us she was doing the best that she could. The only thing left was to read a quote that would lead us into dinner.

Earlier, I had been given Karen's book of Outward Bound-related quotes. There were hundreds and hundreds of them. I was determined to identify exactly the right set of words that would unify this group. I paused on a Winnie-the-Pooh quote but dismissed it for being too cutesy. I hesitated on a Thoreau quote but dismissed it as being too outdoorsy. I scanned my eyes over the Chinese Proverbs but dismissed them as being far too vague.

And then, there it was.

Before me stood the Golden Ticket quote of all quotes: the last verse to "Closer to Fine" by the Indigo Girls.

When I saw those words on the page, I actually gasped and got a bit choked up. That song has buoyed me through more difficult times in my life than I could possibly describe. I sang it in my senior talent show years ago and my siblings used it as their dedication quote to me in my high school yearbook advertisement ("The best thing you ever did for me / Is to help take my life less seriously"). "Closer to Fine" is a song as close to the core of my being as any set of words in the English language. That those lyrics were right there in Karen's book of quotes was nothing less than a prophecy fulfilled.

It also was instantly clear to me that there was no way I was going to recite lyrics from an Indigo Girls song. You don't speak Indigo Girls lyrics; you sing them. So I sang them. Some in the group sang along, and when I sang the last line ("The closer I am to fine"), I instructed them to repeat the line in whatever harmony they could muster. And they did. Now, I don't know that the harmony we created was Carnegie Hall-worthy, but that's not what we needed in that moment. What we needed was to feel closer to fine and that moment magically did indeed bring us closer to something that certainly resembled fine.

Tonight was to be another first: we resolved to ditch the tarps and sleep under the stars. We have been blessed with nothing but cloudless skies since we entered the backcountry and tonight looked to be more of the same clear skies. I'm lying here on my sleeping pallet with my headlamp, alternating between writing and staring up at a complete blanket of stars. The ground beneath me is absurdly uneven, but I'm hoping for a smooth last day tomorrow.

Day 8
June 21, 2015

Yeah, I barely slept. It really was amazing sleeping under the stars, but it would have been better had there been actual sleeping. But actual sleeping would have required a surface that was even remotely conducive to actual sleeping and that was a surface I did not have underneath me last night.

Our wake-up time was 5:45 a.m. We needed to have breakfast, pack up camp, and hit the trail by 6:45 a.m. On this last day hiking out of the backcountry, leaders were not assigned. Instead, Karen asked whether a few people would be willing to volunteer to lead us out of the wilderness and into our van. I heard two people volunteer. One of them was No Trail Name Lady. The other, surprisingly, was a voice that sounded suspiciously like my own. Wait a second—that *was* my voice!

I felt like I had a ton to prove after the debacle that took place under my co-leadership yesterday. The irony that I would be co-leading with No Trail Name Lady on this last day was not lost on me. Thankfully, this was supposed to be a pretty straightforward day and the vibe of the group felt infinitely much improved from yesterday's angst.

We hit the trail at 7:05 a.m., which is the least late we have been all week. Given all the climbing we did at the start of our journey, the hike down to the road was predictably downhill and unpredictably less challenging than our instructors had led us to believe it would be when describing the hike at breakfast. It was a short hike but even after only a few steps, there was a palpable feeling that we were done. We wanted the packs off our backs and we wanted some semblance of cleanliness. The anticipation of a hot shower (I'm gross), a working toilet (I'm so over using a trowel to dig a hole), and clean clothes (the fabric that is covering my skin needs to be burned) quickened our step.

I was near the front of the pack and I jumped out in front for the last mile. We stopped frequently to let the group catch up, but when we knew the road was only a few hundred yards away, Llama, Raven, and I completely ignored the requests to wait up. We were done and the thought of pausing was not even close to an option. This didn't bring us any closer to a shower, but we were desperate to feel the ground under our feet transform from the dirt of the backcountry to the asphalt that would take us back to our base camp. We steeled ourselves for an onslaught of protests at our breaking away from the group, but everyone was so happy to reach that concrete transition point that smiles conquered any sense of fight that may have been felt.

Before heading back to base camp, we walked around an old marble mining facility that was adjacent to the road leading to the backcountry. In other circumstances, this would be the field trip that would have me at my maximum capacity for boredom, ranking even above that middle school trip to see the Intrepid. But this old mining facility had a working toilet, so it was the best field trip of all the field trips. Take that, big, stupid *Intrepid*! (Also, go Team USA in all circumstances and, to all those members of our armed forces, thank you for your service).

When I was waiting in line to use the restroom, I read an informational sign all about the history of the mill site. It turns out that the marble from this mine was used to create both the Tomb of the Unknown Soldier as well as the entire exterior of the Lincoln Memorial. I thought that was actually pretty damn nifty, well, at least until the bathroom became available and then my caring factor went down significantly.

Our last real physical task for the day was to climb the 1.6 miles straight back up that steep hill that led to our base camp. But there was a bit of a twist: we could go up at our own pace and not have to wait for anyone behind us. This was a personal journey up the hill, not a group exercise. Rock Rabbit took off at a run with Sweetie Pie and Tripod not far behind. The rest of us set a brisk walking pace, but even seven days after acclimating to the altitude, that climb was not easy. We huffed and puffed but soldiered steadily up the hill.

At the end of the road, about a third-of-a-mile past our base camp, there was a rapidly moving stream. The optional challenge was to immerse yourself in the 35 degree water. One after one, I watched my groupmates strip down and submerge themselves in the water. I put one foot in the water and learned how cold 35 degrees really is. Turns out: it's really cold.

The only individuals by the stream who had not taken the plunge were Canon and me. We looked at each other, clasped hands, and went in together. Every time I look at pictures on Facebook of people doing those Polar Plunges right after New Year's, I always think, *What a bunch of morons!* Now, I felt like one of those morons. It was an awesome experience and I am beyond glad that I took the plunge. That said, I was not glad (or moronic) enough to accept the challenge to do it a second time when the option was offered.

I should pause here and note that No Trail Name Lady was with us neither for the walk up the hill nor for the icy dip. As soon as it was announced that we could climb up the hill at our own pace, the immediate implication was that she would be left behind. So that's a tricky thing, right? On the one hand, so much of this week was about the group and we were blatantly leaving one person behind. We had been so careful not to leave any micro-trash on the trail and here we were leaving an entire member of our team behind.

On the other hand, much as I embrace the precept that you are only as strong as your weakest link, if you had the opportunity to subtract that link for just a few hours so that the group could fly free, would you? Or is it even the same group anymore? I feel like a complete ass writing that, but that was my reality. We had such an incredible moment at the icy stream and there was no feeling that the experience was dulled by the absence of one member of our group. Does that make us villains? Or does it just make us people who were where they needed to be at that moment surrounded by the people they needed around them? And, yeah, I feel like a complete ass writing that last line, too.

The group then walked back to base camp to clean all of our equipment and return all the gear provided to us. This might not seem like a process worth noting, but it really is a critical part of this journey. There is a type of closure that is provided by cleaning the backpacks, scrubbing the bowls, and refilling iodine bottles. Beware of any trip in which the staff takes care of those tasks for you. We all need to be responsible for returning what was given to us in the condition in which it was given.

It is an inappropriate transfer of energy to let someone else do that for you.

The big surprise came when we learned that we weren't the only group on their last day at base camp. A group of eight fifteen- to eighteen-year olds were just finishing their fifteen-day(!) mountaineering expedition. Karen created an opportunity for our group and their group to sit in a circle and individually share a highlight of our respective trips. Within the first few words of the first teenager sharing, it became clear that the teenagers rocked and our group was lame. I don't mean to diminish our time in the wilderness, but seriously, they rocked and we were lame. These teens spent their first week camping in the snow, survived multiple hailstorms, and yesterday, to finish things off, they did the Tyrolean Traverse, the repelling and, oh yeah, they threw in a ten-mile run as their final personal challenge. In contrast, we walked up the hill. And we took a few breaks on the way up. Again, I don't mean to diminish our accomplishments, but they rocked and we were lame.

The teenagers' stories were so inspiring. One young woman was seeking solitude away from a family in complete turmoil. One young man was questioning whether outdoor education should be the basis for his entire future. And one young superhero was venturing outside New York City for the first time in his life in the most epic way possible. They were all incredible. I am so far from a paid spokesperson for Outward Bound, but every teen should be required to do this. Every one of them.

After we separated from the teens, our group of educators gathered around the campfire for our last dinner together as a group. It was pretty darn lovely. We were all laughing and smiling and hugging. The end was most certainly drawing near and we all knew it.

I signed up to clean dishes after dinner. This was a role for which I had volunteered many times throughout this trip; it felt like an extension of my time in Uganda and it was a task that brought me comfort. Tonight, there was no such comfort to be found.

About three dishes in, my leg completely seized up and started hurting far worse than it previously had all week long. I hobbled over to the rest of the group around the campfire and asked whether someone could take the rest of my shift (thanks, Scribe!). I then climbed into the loft of the lodge to lie down. My leg pain didn't go away when I sprawled out, and I was dreading climbing back down to the campfire outside for a skit that groups traditionally do for the Outward Bound staff in advance of our final closing circle. But Karen being Karen, knowing I was hurting, moved the entire group up to the loft so I didn't have to come down. It was a tiny gesture, but the kindness was enormous.

As soon as the group came up to the loft, I requested to please sit out the skit. At least, I meant it to be a request even as I didn't really allow for the possibility for someone to tell me no. I honestly didn't know what it was that we were supposed to do for the skit and my entertainer/improv hat was most certainly not on my head at that point. I knew I was coming across as more than a bit of a wet blanket, but I really was hurting. The show went on and my understudy debuted to riotous laughter; one person's arms through another person's torso never fails to amuse.

Our last activity was a pinning ceremony in which we all received Outward Bound pins signifying our participation and achievement. The pins apparently are conversation starters when seen by other Outward Bound graduates. It is a secret society of sorts, one that includes Senator Mark Udall, a former executive director of Outward Bound, who often sports the very same pin I was about to receive.

Karen read some inspiring quotes and told us how proud of us she was. The pins were on the floor in the center of our circle surrounding Karen's book of quotes. As we went to the circle to claim our pin, we were given the opportunity to say a few words about what the pin symbolized and voice any commitments it represented for the individual who would proudly be wearing it. When my time arrived to grab my pin, Karen asked whether I wanted her to grab it for me as I was visibly wincing, but grabbing that pin from the ground was something that I really wanted to do for myself. I told the group that the pin symbolized an effort to be more kind to myself and that it would be a reminder that I am in control of telling my own story. As I affixed the pin to my shirt, I shared that I no longer felt like I had to share the parts of my story that were painful. And I truly meant it.

After the ceremony dispersed, I sprawled out in the loft as the night drew to a blurry close. I downed a few Benadryl to make sure that my last night in a sleeping bag featured actual sleep. I removed the pin from my shirt and affixed it to my ever-present satchel so that I could stare at it as I fell asleep. That pin will be the last thing I see tonight and that feels right.

Day 9 (+100)

June 22, 2015 (and also, September 30, 2015)

I'm off the trails, out of the backcountry, and away from the base camp. Kitty is gone, trail names have been forgotten, and now people have gone back to calling me Ken. My adventure in the Colorado Rocky Mountains seems like a hundred days ago. Also, my adventure in the Colorado Rocky Mountains actually *was* a hundred days ago. It has taken me three months to sit down and finally pen this entry.

I've been avoiding writing this conclusion until it was absolutely screaming at me to be written. And not just screaming, but screaming at such a shrill, fevered pitch that the only way to shut it the fuck up was to sit down and purge these words onto paper. So much has happened since Day 8; Outward Bound changed me in ways I never could have anticipated, both physically and emotionally. But first, let's start with that actual last morning.

Our official wake-up call was set for 7:30 a.m. but there wasn't a single member of our group who wasn't up before then. There was a current of pure and utter anxiousness running through base camp: a drive to get our personal gear all packed up, a desire to return to our lives, a trepidation about what saying good-bye would look like, and an overall feeling of being ready. Sure, we were ready to leave Outward Bound behind, but everyone was also commenting how they were ready to apply what they learned to both their teaching and their overall lives.

As we packed, the sun shone brightly and it was another cloudless sky. The weather the entire week was nothing short of a Hanukkah miracle. On the first two days of our trip, it rained heavily, but those were the days that we spent at base camp with access to the weather-protected Dining Lodge for all of us to conduct activities and for one of us to sleep in. (Hi! That would be me). From the minute we strapped the industrial-sized packs onto our backs and headed into the wilderness, nary a cloud floated in the sky above us. Truly: Not. One. Single. Cloud. It's hard to be as appreciative as I think I should be for this miraculous weather—again, those high school kids had to dig campsites in the snow as the hail pelted down on them only four days before our group arrived. I don't have the comparable experience of slogging through the rain or snow. But I do have a keen sense that it all would have been harder to manage with wet things. Dry and sunny gear was most certainly a good thing. A really good thing.

The group ate a quick breakfast, but not all together. We were all doing our own thing: packing, writing down contact information for each other, cleaning the kitchen, and looking out at the mountains. My hip felt a bit better this morning, unquestionably a healing partially fueled by the adrenaline of leaving. I flitted about, helping here and there, staring off into the distance, and hugging people who were strangers a few days ago.

Before long, by about 9:00 a.m., we were all set and ready to go. All that was left was one more walk down the steep hill from base camp to where the van sat ready to whisk us away. The descent was somewhere between race-walking and skipping. We were buoyant, joyful, and smiling. Those smiles faded a bit as soon as we rounded a bend and saw the van. This was it. Outward Bound was over. It was time to say good-bye.

Well, sorta.

This farewell split us back into two parts; the group of us who met in that hotel lobby seven days ago had a four-plus hour trip in front of us back to Denver, while everyone else lived within a thirty-minute drive of the bottom of that hill. This separation was such a weird feeling, a separation in the group that was geographically mandated but emotionally arbitrary.

For the denizens who have resided in Christmas Village, this meant a split right down the middle: Kitty and Canon would be climbing into the van while Llama and Raven would be getting into their own personal vehicles. The good-byes quickly got emotional.

I hugged Llama first. She was my laughing partner, my teacher-of-knots, and most certainly my rock. No, she never did carry my pack, but she certainly made my load infinitely lighter throughout this adventure. After all of the other Sharks had been hugged, Llama and I locked eyes again and there was no other possible outcome in life than to come back together and hug one more time. Truly an amazing woman.

And speaking of amazing women: Karen. I'm not quite sure what I can possibly write about Karen. Although my good-byes to the residents of Christmas Village were chock-full of emotion, saying good-bye to Karen was when I got all choked up and the tears started flowing. I just want to *be* Karen. There's really no other way to say it. She was the culmination of all these different adventures, the last step in the Darwinian mentorship evolution that started with Gloria in Uganda, continued with Mary at Esalen, and now was standing before me at the base of one of the Colorado Rocky Mountains. From Gloria, I learned a bit about how to get stuff done and make a difference with a drive and zeal that produces actual life-saving results. From Mary, I learned a bit about how to heal and cut through all the self-created artifice and Defenses that exist to keep me in a constant state of pain and turmoil.

From Karen, well, it's almost difficult to wrap my mind around what I learned. She certainly nudged me infinitely closer to living in the present and distancing myself from narratives that never fail to make me sad. She certainly elbowed me infinitely closer to increasing my confidence and believing that I could scale any mountain before me. She certainly pushed me infinitely closer to believing that I have a unique voice to share and that it was only my fear of critics unknown and unavoidable that never fails to hold me back.

I just want to *be* Karen. There's really no other way to say it.

After the last of the Sharks had hugged the last of the Jets, it was time to go. Canon, Scribe, Tripod, Rock Rabbit, Sweetie Pie, No Trail Name Lady, and I piled into the van and waved good-bye as half the group left the other half behind. Again, it was such a weird feeling to be split up like that. Although I had a vague memory of starting out in two separate groups, any previously felt van-group-pride now seemed silly.

We Jets chatted amiably until we reached that point where it was clear that we had re-entered civilization and, thus, cell phone coverage. Without question, I was the most guilty of burying my focus in my phone both first and for the longest. Although I really and truly did not spend as much time as I would normally spend surfing around online, it was embarrassing that I was spending any time online at all. The embarrassment didn't stop me from doing it, but it was extremely significant that the embarrassment was present at all. What up, Progress?

There was some talk in the van about grabbing a bite to eat together when we arrived in Denver. I wasn't flying back to Cleveland until the following day, so I certainly had time on my hands. Tripod said he wasn't able to go to lunch as he had to get home. Canon said she wasn't able to go to lunch as she was meeting her sister. No Trail Name Lady obviously wasn't going to go to lunch given her disconnect with the group this week. So that left Sweetie Pie, Scribe, Rock Rabbit, and me to grab a burrito.

Oh, and also, No Trail Name Lady came with us. It honestly didn't even occur to me that she would want to join us: I knew she had a family to get back to and there was also the part where we just hadn't really gotten along for the past eight days or so. But I certainly wasn't going to object to her lunching with us.

I wished that I had objected. I wouldn't have. But I still wished that I had objected.

No Trail Name Lady was a fount of negative energy when we arrived in Denver. I'm not exactly Ollie Optimism, but there was the part where I had just completed Outward Freakin' Bound, so I did have a bit of a sense of completion. It was difficult to embrace this sense of completion as No Trail Name Lady sat in the backseat of the car highlighting all the murders that had happened in Denver while we were gone, complaining about how far we had parked from the burrito place, kvetching about how there weren't any seats outside that weren't in direct sunlight, and bemoaning, lamenting, and grumbling about myriad other things.

I was torn on how to respond. On the one hand, all the stressors of backpacking in the Colorado Rocky Mountains were gone, so my tolerance for enduring this negativity was significantly higher. On the other hand, the obligation to mutually support your fellow Outward Bound travelers regardless of their emotional state was also gone, so my tolerance for enduring this negativity was significantly lower. Ultimately, figuring out how to respond was a fairly moot point as it turned out to be a pretty quick meal before No Trail Name Lady left us to rejoin her family.

Rock Rabbit, Sweetie Pie, Scribe, and I decided to go for ice cream. There was almost no topic of conversation other than No Trail Name Lady and navigating the week with her. After ice cream, Rock Rabbit left us to see his parents and we met up with Sweetie Pie's husband, the staff member for Outward Bound. There was almost no topic of conversation other than No Trail Name Lady and navigating the week with her. We then parted ways and I met up with a cyclist I had befriended years ago on AIDS/LifeCycle. There was almost no topic of conversation other than No Trail Name Lady and navigating the week with her. Later on in the night, Scribe ended up crashing in my hotel room as she was flying out the following day as well. In that hotel room, there was almost no topic of conversation other than No Trail Name Lady and navigating the week with her.

Scribe and I went to bed early, headed to the airport first thing the next morning, and parted ways. That was it. Nobody left to hug. Nobody left to bid adieu. Outward Bound and this adventure were over. When I settled into my seat on the plane to pen this last entry, the fact that the subject of No Trail Name Lady dominated every conversation I had in Denver smacked into me. And let's correct the passive voice here: I not only let the subject of No Trail Name Lady dominate every conversation, but I was very much a ringmaster in the circus where I filled all three rings with No Trail Name Lady.

What was I doing? Seriously, what on Earth was I doing? I had this once-in-a-life experience climbing upside-down across rivers and repelling down cliffs and scaling mountains and going to the bathroom outside (that last one, incidentally, was just as big in my mind as the other feats) and I was actively diminishing my experience by solely couching it in terms of a Negative Nancy who I would likely never again encounter in this mortal coil. Yet even as I chastised myself, I had this unshakable feeling that I would continue to put No Trail Name Lady at the foreground of my Colorado retellings both orally to those who knew me and written on these pages. Thus, sitting on that plane on a runway in Denver, I put my pen down and resolved to write this final entry at a later date.

Only, I didn't think it would take me roughly a hundred days to get back here. That colossal spate of time can be traced back to two root causes. First, as the Confucian bumper stickers sagely tell us: life happens. The dog days of summer plus finding the guy of my dreams plus the start of a new semester plus losing the guy of my dreams plus grading papers plus getting the guy of my dreams back into my life: well, that equation only served to equal the sum of "not writing." That's the easy root cause to call out, and I wish that were the only reason why these words didn't get written.

Far more significant was the other root cause: my avoidance. Sitting here writing these words is nothing short of overwhelming. There are four-ton weights of expectation tied to my ankles that have caused me to sink down to the ocean floor of that body of water called "Lake Meaning Making." I feel like I not only have to make sense of my adventure in Colorado, but I also have to tie it together with some greater universal meaning that brings together Uganda Act #1, the bike ride, Esalen, and Uganda Act #2. For the past hundred days, I have let that pressure drown me until I reached a breaking point when these words finally had to get out of my skull and onto the page. It was finally time for *Mutebi* to come up for air.

To make it a might bit easier on myself, I thought it would be helpful to return to the Ken Schneck Manifesto of Expectations that I created at the start of my Colorado journey.

Expectation #1 – I can handle the physicality of this trip.

Verdict – Yes. And No. There was nothing physical that I didn't do in Colorado. The one activity I skipped (sliding down that snow bank) was due to the emotional exhaustion having scaled that summit, not a physical limitation. But I definitely was in pain a good part of the trip and I chalked it up to my not being hiking-ready.

Turns out, not so! There actually *was* something wrong with me. After seeing a few doctors in Cleveland, an MRI was finally ordered that clearly displayed "Spinal Stenosis with Neural Claudication." Yeah, I didn't know what that was either. The third time the surgeon explained it, I was able to understand that I apparently have a congenitally narrow spinal column that was being almost completely obstructed by some wayward discs who wanted to take an adventure of their own away from their base camp. Thus, nerves weren't able to travel down my legs. Thus, the intense pain.

You'll notice that I used the word surgeon. That's because I had surgery. A laminectomy. The newest permanent tattoo on my body is a three-inch scar on my lower back from where I was opened up so that said surgeon could remove vertebra from my back and shave away some discs. It's a surgery normally meant for fifty-five- to eighty-year olds. At thirty-eight, I consider myself to be an overachiever in the world of laminectomies. Far more important, there actually was something physically wrong with me on that trip, which oddly made me a feel a bit better. I wasn't just emotionally rejecting parts of that adventure, it was a physical rejection too.

Expectation #2 – eight days away from social media—the longest I have probably gone since Prodigy crashed on our Apple IIe (look it up, kids) —will be a freeing experience.

Verdict: It rocked. And I probably can't do it again. I recognize my online addiction and my efforts to curb its use are all for naught except when I go to Uganda, pedal my bike, go to a healing retreat, or backpack in the mountains. That just means I need to book more adventures!

Expectation #3 – It's not going to rain.

Verdict: When it mattered, it didn't rain. See above.

Expectation #4 – I will not get a single blister. Not one single blister the entirety of the trip no matter how new these boots are, even in the unlikely scenario in which I just bought them a few days ago which I, y'know, did.

Verdict: I didn't get a single blister. Princess Podiatry really was a goddess of a tripmate and my feet were so grateful for her ministrations. Also, please don't buy new boots a few days before you go backpacking for eight days. It's really not a smart thing to do. I realize that now.

Expectation #5 – Pooping in the woods will be a piece of cake.

Verdict: I'm embarrassed that this was such a concern for me, even as I totally get why it held that place of importance. I'm happy to report that everything went just fine. Let's move on.

Expectation #6 – There will be cake.

Verdict: There wasn't. But those dark chocolate M&Ms at the top of Marble Mountain were far better than cake. And Karen treated us to any number of fried items in camp, so I was not missing any type of confection.

Expectation #7 – I'm going to get something out of this, a break-through I didn't know I needed, an insight I didn't anticipate, a revela-tion of epic proportions that will stay with me for all the days to come.

Verdict: I'm a moron.

In looking back at all of these adventures, I somehow get stranded in the middle ground between being present and trying to figure out the meaning in every Ugandan orphan, every piece of gravel under my bike, every sea lion in California, and every mountain in Colorado. I exist partly in the activity before me and partly in the wonderful world of, "But what does it all mean?" I have these incredible interactions with Gloria, Mary, and Karen, but then I obsess over them to the point where I'm not even sure what we were talking about to begin with. I don't want to take these experiences for granted, but I also don't want to move them completely from reality into interpretations that only make sense in my own head.

Here at the end, there are a few things I know for certain.

I am certain that I want more adventure. I want to find more of these multiday experiences and sit down at the end of each day, pen in hand, and write about my journeys. Aside from my dissertation (which was half the word count of these journals), these adventures are the only reliable triggers that get me writing. And I'm happier when I'm writing.

I am certain that there is not a ton that separates me from No Trail Name Lady. There was so much lacking in confidence that I never expressed because she did it for me. I repeat: there is not a ton that separates me from No Trail Name Lady.

I am certain that I need reminders of life lessons. Colorado Karen told me things that Esalen Mary had already told me. The bike ride taught me things Uganda had already taught me. One adventure provided me with experiences that another one had already provided. I am not closed off to learning, but I also may need to be provided the lesson a second time. Also, a third and a fourth time wouldn't hurt. I promise: it will absolutely stick by the fifth time. *(Disclaimer: it might not.)*

Above all, I am certain I don't know the answers. I had to take a deep breath after writing that sentence. As a snarky gay Jew who didn't grow up having adventures, I have lived cerebrally for so long that I think I should be able to figure out how these adventures affect my life.

I can't.

I have a greater appreciation for Uganda and all that goes into nonprofit work that can lift up lives (with their own distinct cultures) on the other side of the world. Biking has become one of my favorite centering practices in my life, as long-distance rides are now one of the only activities that allow my mind to go quiet in the face of the societal tumult around me. Esalen enabled me to be able to admit that it's actually <gasp> okay to not be okay. And Colorado taught me about the three concentric circles of comfort, change, and panic: you can only change when you make yourself uncomfortable, but go too far, and you are firmly in the circle of panic. That's not a productive place to live.

There are more journeys in front of me, more adventures to be had. There is *Tulibaluganda* to be explored in new places and sea lions to be discovered in unfamiliar lands. I just need to be open to it all. And I think I can actually be successful. If I keep putting one foot in front of the other, slowly but surely, I will continue to move forward.

Just one foot in front of the other.

Over and over again.

Rinse and repeat.

Sometimes, well . . . sometimes, it really is just that easy.

ACKNOWLEDGMENTS

Christine Deegan: Your voicemail message gave me the confidence to move this project forward. I will be forever grateful for those forty-three seconds and for your friendship.

Matthew Chojnacki: You and **1984 Publishing** came into my life at the exact moment when I thought these words would never be printed. I am supremely grateful for your skill, trust, and belief that this all would be worth reading.

Laura Wimbels: You are a publishing enabler. Thank you for making that key introduction and for capturing my soul in your photography.

Dave Perillo: I smile from ear to ear every time I look at the artwork you created for this book. You are talent incarnate.

Heather Taylor: Thanks to you and **Blue Heron Images & Words** for making my words stronger and my meaning clearer with every track change.

Thanks to My Cleveland Heroes: **Sean Watterson** and **The Happy Dog** for providing my stories with a home; **Gypsy Beans & Baking Company** for providing me with the caffeinated haven to write; **Megan Kuhar** and **heypoletti! recordings** for expertly recordings my words and giving me a place on the web; **Bella Sin** and **Ohio Burlesque** for the stage and the pasties; and **Zachariah Durr**, **Adam Richard** and **Keep Talking: A Storytelling Show** for repeatedly giving me a microphone and for providing Cleveland with a storytelling nirvana.

Suzanne Kingsbury: From the very start, your advice and direction steered me as straight as I am capable of sailing. Thank you for being every bit the Book Shaman that the entire **Gateless Writing Community** knows you to be.

Smith Publicity: Thanks to **Corrine Moulder**, **Mike Onorato**, and especially **Andrea Kiliany Thatcher** for the hard work and excellent new contacts.

Becca Ritterspach: You were there for every step of this process. Thank you for the Westminster Kennel Club Dog Show viewing, your macaroon angst, and your unwavering support.

Annette, Carlye, Debra, Diana, Christie, Erin, Gina, Jack, Jamie, Keith, Laura, Shannon, Susan, Sky, and all of the superstars who surround me: I am beyond fortunate to have friends who inspire and amuse me. You all lift me up, keep me smiling, and push me to do more. Also, if I didn't list your name, it just means I got choked up even typing it out, but know that I was thinking about you really, really hard.

Stefie, Missy, Joel, Dave, Cory, Joy, Sammy, Leah, Lindsay, Jilly, Sara, Carson, and Jessica: It's not a hora without you.

Barry and **Terri Schneck**: In each interaction we have ever had, you manage to be proud of me, bewildered by me, amused by me, and demand more from me. I am emotionally and genetically nothing without you.

And, finally, **Rich Hinkelman**: When we first met, you told me I had a lot of stories. It awes and humbles me that you continued to listen to them.